SWEET LAND OF LIBERTY?

Books by Henry Mark Holzer

Sweet Land of Liberty?
Government's Money Monopoly
The Gold Clause

SWEET LAND OF LIBERTY?

The Supreme Court and Individual Rights

by Henry Mark Holzer

The Common Sense Press, Inc.
Costa Mesa, California

This book is dedicated to

AYN RAND, *qua* political philosopher

TABLE OF CONTENTS

FOREWORD

As we review the progress of our nation from the vantage point of the final years of the twentieth century, two things stand in stark contrast—on one hand, the immense technological leaps of scientists and technicians have provided a higher standard of living to the masses than even the richest kings of history could enjoy; on the other hand, the nation's social structure is in a state of turmoil so deep that many observers feel collapse is imminent. The reason for technological progress seems self-evident. The reason for the lack of progress in the social arena is widely unknown.

I believe that our social problems result from man's long misunderstanding of individual freedom. Individual freedom could be defined as the state that exists when an individual is free to choose, without interference, what disposition he will make of the things that he produces or honestly acquires. To the extent that other individuals use force or fraud to interfere with an individual's freedom, that is, to take his goods, or restrict his right to freely exchange those goods with others, chaos and conflict inevitably follow. While almost all societies believe that *one individual* should not be allowed to directly interfere with the life or property of another individual (laws against theft, fraud, and murder, for example, exist in almost all societies), conversely, the great majority in every culture believes that *the state* should be allowed to do so, for the "good" of society as a whole.

I believe that future historians will someday identify the single, great philosophical premise that has formed the foundation for social stagnation and decay, and has condemned this nation and all nations before it to an endless repetition of the devastating cycles of inflation, depression, revolution, and war. This destructive premise is simple, and deeply ingrained in all cultures on earth today. It is that *the individual of any group, tribe, or nation must place his interests beneath the "needs" of the collective.* In other words, the self-interest of the individual is secondary to the interest of the state, and therefore the state is always justified in controlling any individual's actions, or taking any of his goods, whenever the state, in its own judgement, decides that this is in the "best interests" of the community as a whole.

The intellectual leaders of the American Revolution recognized the inherent dangers of allowing the state unbridled power to control the life and property of individual citizens—these dangers were clearly evidenced by the overt intrusions of the British government against the colonists. For a brief moment on earth, the premise that the good of society as determined by the ruling political body was a claim on the life and property of every citizen was challenged. The Declaration of Independence took the bold and nearly unprecedented stand that individuals had certain "unalienable rights," among which were life, liberty, and the pursuit of happiness, and that the function of government was confined to securing those rights for individuals. In other words, the purpose of government was not to regulate, control, and plunder individuals for the benefit of the collective, but rather to make certain that each individual enjoyed personal freedom from the encroachments of others.

The U.S. Constitution was to be the framework for the new nation. It was an architectural plan for a new type of government, a kind of protective agency that would insure the liberty of the citizens within its domain. Many critics, however, saw through the rhetoric, and realized that the document itself was a sweeping grant of almost unlimited power to a central body of elected "representatives" (politicians). Aware that a tyranny of the majority could be every bit as oppressive of individual liberty as a tyranny of a tyrant king, these critics demanded the Constitution be amended to provide a set of clearly defined limitations on the power of this new government to encroach on the freedom of individuals. The first ten amendments to the Constitution became known as the "Bill of Rights." These enumerated rights, including the freedom to speak, write, assemble, petition, bear arms, practice any religion, and be secure against being deprived of life, liberty, or property without due process of law, were (or so the framers thought) clearly and unequivocally spelled out. Today, every child in school is indoctrinated with these ideas, and the overwhelming majority of American citizens fully believes that these rights remain intact and inviolable.

The Supreme Court of the United States was created by the Constitution and given the ultimate authority to sit in judgement on all cases arising under the Constitution. This court, then, became the ultimate judge of all conflicts between the state and the individual. Its mandate is the Constitution itself. Its task: to determine, in each case, if laws passed or actions taken by any branch of government, local, state, or federal, violate the guarantees of individual freedoms set forth in the Constitution.

In *Sweet Land of Liberty?*, Professor Henry Mark Holzer presents a remarkable documentation of the history of Supreme Court decisions regarding individual liberty. What he has discovered is that far from upholding the intent of the framers of the Constitution, the Supreme Court has consistently, throughout its history, weighed each case not against the standard of inviolable individual rights, but rather against a completely different standard—the standard of community interests. In other words, the highest court does not ask the question, "is this action by government violating the freedom of this individual?" but rather, "is this violation of individual freedom by government justified because it's in the best interests of the community?"

This is no small distinction. Once the "best interests of the community" become the standard by which individual actions are judged, then freedom ceases to exist. The best interests of the community are, by definition, determined by the majority, and are carried out by the people they put in office. If the majority determines that women will not show their faces in public, then women will wear veils. If it determines that certain books will be banned, then those books will disappear. If the majority determines that blacks will be slaves, blacks will be slaves. If it determines that Jews should be gassed, then Jews will be gassed. There is no such thing as individual liberty once the premise is accepted that the majority opinion should determine what is best for the community.

Every social ill of society is rooted in the abuse of individual freedom. If a better world is the objective, then there must be a growing understanding of the nature of liberty, and the means by which people are deprived of it. Our culture teaches us that we live in a free country, and that our freedoms are guaranteed to us by the Constitution. So strong is this message, that we believe it even in the face of absolute evidence to the contrary. A stunning example of the effectiveness of this delusion appeared in the nation's press in 1982. Mark Schmucker, 22, a Mennonite, believes that draft registration violates the laws of Christ, and refused to register rather than act contrary to his religious beliefs. He was indicted and convicted. So effective was the cultural indoctrination, however, that even as the jail cell door closed behind him his final comment was, "I'm proud to live in a country with religious freedom." Unfortunately, it was not an attempt at sarcasm. It's time that we stop deluding ourselves, and accept the facts as they exist. What is needed is a body of literature that defines individual freedom, clearly shows its extreme importance and relevance to our lives, and exposes all encroachments on that freedom. *Sweet Land of Liberty?* is a very significant addition to that body of work. I sincerely hope that it will be widely read today, and that someday it will be regarded by historians as one of the parts of the intellectual catalyst that created the society dreamed of by the leaders of the American Revolution: a society of true individual liberty.

John A. Pugsley

ACKNOWLEDGMENTS

No book comes to life without the author receiving help from other people. Though the nature of their assistance usually differs, each person in his or her own way contributes something. So, too, with this book, written while I was on sabbatical from Brooklyn Law School. As always, Erika Holzer's editing was incisive and contributed immeasurably to my efforts. Ingrid Celms, my secretary at Brooklyn Law School, cheerfully and capably produced a typed manuscript so perfect that readers from coast to coast have described it as the best they have ever seen. My agent, Meredith Bernstein of New York City, understood the book's importance from the beginning, and indefatigably submitted it to publishers who did not. Dyanne Petersen made the crucial introduction, at the right time. Carol Cardwell, patient beyond the call of duty, and the rest of the staff at Common Sense Press, has efficiently and with unfailing courtesy and goodwill transformed my manuscript into an actual hardcover book. Lastly, I must speak of my publisher, John A. Pugsley. To say that Jack made a "contribution" to *Sweet Land of Liberty?* is to understate considerably. He made it possible. Nothing less. His appreciation of the book's value, his willingness to act on his judgment, and his style and integrity in doing so, are attributes which I deeply respect and will always be grateful for. In an important sense, if *Sweet Land of Liberty?* has any influence on our culture, Jack Pugsley will have been much of the reason.[*]

---

[*] There is one more important acknowledgment that must be made. Ordinarily, I would have done so above, but circumstances are such that I am certain the individual involved would prefer to remain anonymous. Suffice to say that I am deeply grateful to one other person whose understanding and graciousness made it possible for this book to be published now.

INTRODUCTION

It is vain, sir, to extenuate the matter. The gentlemen may cry, Peace, peace! but there is no peace. The war has actually begun. The next gale that sweeps from the north will bring to our ears the clash of resounding arms! Our brethren are already in the field! Why stand we here idle? What is it that the gentlemen wish? What would they have? Is life so dear or peace so sweet as to be purchased at the price of chains and slavery? Forbid it, Almighty God. I know not what course others may take, but as for me, give me liberty or give me death.

—Patrick Henry

As a child I was taught, in school and out, that the United States of America was a free country.

Not an uncommon perception, even today. Most Americans, if reminded of Patrick Henry's stirring words, will have an emotional response equivalent to: We made it! We do have liberty!

After all, we have a written Constitution and Bill of Rights. The Constitution expressly prohibits states from interfering with contracts. People can say what they wish—the First Amendment of the Bill of Rights guarantees that, and freedom of religion, too. The Fifth and Fourteenth Amendments assure that no one will be deprived of property without due process and equal protection of the laws. Other constitutional safeguards protect Americans in many additional ways. We've developed a two-party system and secret ballot voting. Our federal and state legislatures, our president and governors, and many of our judges, are popularly elected. "Checks and balances" allow chief executives to veto legislation, but legislatures (with enough votes) can override vetoes. Ultimately, legislation can be declared unconstitutional by the judiciary—especially by the Supreme Court of the United States, the highest tribunal in the land and the Constitution's final arbiter.

So, all we have to do, well-meaning Americans think—*I* thought—is uphold our Constitution; then, our liberty will be secure. As a child having been taught these things, I believed America was a free country—especially compared to most others, notably our wartime ally, the communist Soviet Union, and our then enemies, fascist Italy, nazi Germany, and militarist Japan.

Yet, despite reinforcement of this idea through continued schooling and the constant outpourings of patriotism that swept the country in those days, and even though I was only eleven years old, something toward the war's end disquieted me considerably. Though of course I knew that the United States had fielded millions of men and that there were countless eager volunteers, I had never realized that some of the members of the armed forces were serving unwillingly. Not until one day late in 1944, when I overheard my mother and father talking. My father, then well into his thirties, faced being *drafted*. Even an eleven-year-old's grasp of the meaning and implications of that concept—my father being taken away, forced to fight and maybe die—clashed head-on with my rudimentary understanding of liberty. I remember wondering how a country that was supposedly fighting for freedom could take the liberty, and perhaps the life, of an unwilling citizen. Though the family's anxiety soon passed (my father failed his physical: flat feet), that nagging question remained.

In the years that followed, as I became aware of more and more apparent contradictions between how things were supposed to be and how they were, I began to realize that my father's draft problem had exemplified an important principle. I began to realize that merely "upholding" our Constitution was *not* enough to secure our liberty—that we had a Supreme Court to do the upholding for us, and that something was profoundly wrong with the results. The full realization hit me when I entered law school. In every course dealing with the power of government and its delicate relationship to the individual (especially Constitutional Law), it quickly became apparent to me that the freedom I had long taken for granted was largely illusory, and that America was not then (and never had been!) as free as I thought. I learned that much of the blame, ironically, belonged to the ultimate guardian of the Constitution, the Supreme Court of the United States. It wasn't a matter of a *particular* Court in any given period of our history, and it wasn't a matter of *who* was interpreting our Constitution—i.e., whether the Bench was made up of "liberals" or "conservatives," "strict constructionists" or "loose" ones. It was a matter of our Supreme Court *consistently* upholding the constitutionality of laws which violated individual rights*—laws enacted by the many to the detriment of the few, laws designed to implement the values of ever-shifting majority coalitions.

For example:

- Antisodomy laws, criminalizing every form of private consensual sexual conduct, except coitus in a monogamous heterosexual marriage.
- Conscription laws, causing unwilling draftees to be brutalized, maimed and killed.
- Military zone laws, "relocating" loyal Americans of Japanese ancestry from their West Coast homes to desert internment camps.
- Wage and hour laws, requiring private employers to establish pay scales and working conditions mandated, not by the free market and mutual agreement, but by government.
- Legal tender laws, compelling creditors to accept repayment of virtually worthless "greenbacks" instead of the gold that their

---

* Simply put, the principle of individual rights holds that each person is sovereign, that no one has a right to violate that sovereignty by initiating physical force, and that the only basis for relations between people is voluntary consent.

debtors had promised.

- Mortgage moratorium laws, preventing banks from foreclosing defaulted mortgages.

And the list went on, with the Court relentlessly upholding law after law, passed to accomplish what an ever-changing majority wanted, at the expense of the few. The consummate example, of course, was when the Supreme Court of the United States upheld even slavery. Short of literal human sacrifice, there is no more obscene illustration of unbridled majority rule in action than slavery—an utterly rightless status where one human being's very existence hangs on the slender thread of another's caprice. Yet once, in America, slavery had been a constitutionally acceptable institution.

When I finished law school in the late 1950s, I knew for certain that America was not really a free country. I knew what the Court's stated justifications were for consistently upholding legislation inimical to the interests of the individual. I also knew something which, I felt certain, many Americans did not realize—at least not fully: that merely because our Supreme Court labeled some legislative act "constitutional" did *not* mean the act wasn't doing violence to the Constitution—and that, too often, what the Court *was* doing violence to were those personal liberties we had thought so secure. But still I did not feel that I really understood *why*. It seemed to me that an integrating explanation was lacking, that there must be a single principle which would make intelligible why the history of American constitutional law was littered with the casualties of a war whose battles I could study, but whose nature I did not grasp.

Then, in the early 1960s, I came upon the writings of Ayn Rand, the philosopher to whose ideas this book is dedicated. She understood very well the nature of that war, and what had betrayed America's promise of freedom. It was a simple truth:

America's inner contradiction was the altruist-collectivist ethics.*

Before I go any further, a few words are necessary about these two

---

* Ayn Rand, "Man's Rights," *The Virtue of Selfishness* (The New American Library, 1965), p. 127.

ethical concepts because most people have long misunderstood and misused them, and their benign connotations have dangerously obscured their real meaning.

Altruism is popularly taken to mean nothing more than simply being nice to people, e.g., contributing to medical research, helping the poor, supporting the arts. The real meaning of altruism ethically, however, is far different. It is "the doctrine that the general welfare of society is the proper goal of an individual's action," not his or her own happiness.* Rand has stripped the concept down even further to its naked essence, defining altruism as "the ethical theory which regards man as a sacrificial animal, which holds that man has no right to exist for his own sake, that service to others is the only justification of his existence, and that self-sacrifice is his highest moral duty."† Thus, not only does altruism have nothing to do with being nice to people, but we shall see that when it is put into practice the consequences for individual rights are necessarily devastating.

Closely related to the concept of altruism is that of collectivism which, contrary to popular belief, has nothing to do with people inhabiting the same planet or neighborhood, let alone persons with common interests voluntarily coming together. On the contrary, and as antithetically to the concept of individual rights as anything could possibly be, collectivism "holds that the individual has no rights, that his life and work belong to the group (to 'society,' to the tribe, the state, the nation) and that the group may sacrifice him at its own whim to its own interest."‡

Thus, given the real nature of altruism and of collectivism, Rand's identification seemed a plausible explanation of why the decisions of the Supreme Court of the United States, virtually from its first day of existence, consistently failed to protect individual rights. Indeed, the explanation's plausibility was considerably enhanced once I realized something more: that because altruism and collectivism are ethical doctrines, and because the only way to implement them is by force, they necessarily have a familiar political-legal corollary: statism, "the

---

* *Webster's New World Dictionary*, (The World Publishing Company, 1970).

† Ayn Rand, "The Objectivist Ethics," *The Virtue of Selfishness* (The New American Library, 1965), pp. 32-33.

‡ Ayn Rand, "Racism," *The Virtue of Selfishness* (The New American Library, 1965), p. 175.

principle or policy of concentrating extensive economic, political, and related controls in the state at the cost of individual liberty."* Rand explained the relationships this way:

> The dominant ethics of mankind's history were variants of the altruist-collectivist doctrine which subordinated the individual to some higher authority, either mystical or social. Consequently, most political systems were variants of the same statist tyranny, differing only in degree, not in basic principle, limited only by the accidents of tradition, of chaos, of bloody strife and periodic collapse. Under all such systems, morality was a code applicable to the individual, but not to society. Society was placed *outside* the moral law, as its embodiment or source or exclusive interpreter—and the inculcation of self-sacrificial devotion to social duty was regarded as the main purpose of ethics in man's earthly existence.
>
> Since there is no such entity as "society," since society is only a number of individual men, this meant, in practice, that the rulers of society were exempt from moral law; subject only to traditional rituals, they held total power and exacted blind obedience—on the implicit principle of: "The good is that which is good for society (or for the tribe, the race, the nation), and the ruler's edicts are its voice on earth."
>
> This was true of all statist systems, under all variants of the altruist-collectivist ethics, mystical or social. "The Divine Right of Kings" summarizes the political theory of the first—"*Vox populi, vox dei*" of the second. As witness: the theocracy of Egypt, with the Pharaoh as an embodied god—the unlimited majority rule or *democracy* of Athens—the welfare state run by the Emperors of Rome—the Inquisition of the late Middle Ages—the absolute monarchy of France—the welfare state of Bismarck's Prussia—the gas chambers of nazi Germany—the slaughterhouse of the Soviet Union.†

If Rand was correct that "America's inner contradiction was the altruist-collectivist ethics," and if the Court's decisions *were* rooted in those ethics, it would become necessary to add to her list of statist systems the so-called mixed economy of the United States.

Because of the shocking yet seemingly plausible possibility that *in*

---

* *The American College Dictionary*, (Random House, 1957).

† Ayn Rand, "Man's Rights," *The Virtue of Selfishness* (The New American Library, 1965), p. 123.

principle (though not in degree) the ethical-political-legal system of the United States differed little from theocracies, welfare states, monarchies and bloody totalitarian dictatorships, I set out to make a systematic analysis of virtually every major Supreme Court case dealing with individual rights and the exercise of government power. And during the past twenty years as a lawyer, the last ten as a Professor of Law, that is exactly what I have done. The results of that effort are what this book is all about.

Unfortunately, what I have found proved that Rand was correct.

The altruist-collectivist ethics *have* consistently been the motivational base of Supreme Court decision making. As a result, the Court has been far from solicitous of individual rights, choosing instead consistently to uphold ever-increasing government power at the individual's expense.*

To the extent that there has been disagreement between the justices, it has not been over the fundamental principle of whether government *should* control people's lives, but merely over the details of how, when, and to what extent their lives *will* be controlled.

It is not a pleasant story, this relentless violation of individual rights by the principal institution sworn to protect them, this utilization by the Supreme Court of the altruist-collectivist ethics to create a statist government in America. For those who love liberty, each chapter in our story—business, property, contracts, religion, speech, sex, slavery—will painfully reveal just how far we have traveled down that road. But the story must be told, and understood, if we are to halt our nation's headlong rush to the abyss into which all unfree countries must eventually plunge.

We begin with what the Court has inflicted on American business.

---

* Though from time to time and issue to issue some justices may have appeared to care about individual rights, their interest has been both superficial and highly selective. For example, as we shall see, though "liberals" have always opposed government restraints on speech, they have avidly supported government restraints on business; though "conservatives" have always opposed government regulation of property through zoning, they have avidly supported government regulation of abortion.

1.

BUSINESS

... everyone thirsteth after gaine, ...

—*Sir Edward Coke*

In Greek mythology, Prometheus brought fire from heaven to benefit mankind. As punishment, he was chained to a rock by Zeus, where each day a vulture ate at the captive's liver. Throughout most of our nation's history, certainly during the past hundred years, American business has been treated in basically the same way by government. In return for having brought unparalleled prosperity to a small nation starting from scratch, business people have been shackled and bled by government.

Tax laws have removed from productive use capital necessary for reinvestment, diverting it instead to countless special interests. Antitrust and fair-trade laws have contradictorily and impotently attempted to compel competition and protect consumers from themselves. Instead, they have caused business decisions to be predicated, not on marketplace considerations, but on guesses of how bureaucrats and judges would interpret unintelligible laws. Labor laws have created compulsory unionization, with its many attendant problems for unwilling employees and employers—and contributed greatly to America's steady decline as the world's preeminent industrial power.

The ways in which government has controlled, regulated, manipulated, coerced, and otherwise bent American business to its will are indeed many and familiar. Not so familiar, however, is the *motivation* for the way government has treated business. To tell *that* story, I have selected seven cases decided by the Supreme Court of the United States. These seven in particular were chosen over other perhaps better-known cases, not only for what they say about the nature and scope of government control of business, but also because in each one the anti-individual rights premises that animated the decision lay unusually close to the surface and were rather explicit.

Back in 1903, the State of Oregon enacted a law regulating the working hours of women. It provided that: " . . . no female [shall] be employed in any mechanical establishment, or factory, or laundry in this state more than ten hours during any one day."[1]

Today, of course, when social legislation is commonplace, and wage and hour laws an accepted fact of industrial life, the 1903 Oregon statute does not seem unusual. But back then, things were quite different.

One September day in 1905, Mrs. E. Gotcher worked more than ten hours in the Grand Laundry. As a result, its owner was charged with a misdemeanor. Not surprisingly, he was convicted. The conviction, and the law's constitutionality, was upheld in the Oregon courts. The next stop was the Supreme Court of the United States.

There, the question to be decided was whether a woman could choose to work more than a ten-hour day, or whether the state could constitutionally impose its values on employer and employee alike by putting a ceiling on her working hours. As always, underneath the constitutional question lurked an ethical consideration which would really decide the outcome—a consideration involving the nature of government's relation to the individual.

The statute was, of course, upheld—to the cheers of liberals who applauded the Supreme Court's enlightened concern for working women who, allegedly, either did not know, or could not protect, their own interests. But if the decision's partisans (especially women) had paid attention to the Court's *reasons* for its conclusion, they might have felt differently.

The unanimous Court's explanation for *why* it upheld the statute is somewhat lengthy, but well worth setting forth:

> That woman's physical structure and the performance of material functions places her at a disadvantage in the struggle for subsistence is obvious. This is especially true when the burdens of motherhood are upon her. Even when they are not . . . continuance for a long time on her feet at work . . . tends to injurious effects upon the body, and, *as healthy mothers are essential to vigorous offspring, the physical wellbeing of woman becomes an object of public interest and care in order to preserve the strength and vigor of the race.*
>
> *Still again, history discloses the fact that woman has always been dependent upon man.* He established his control at the outset by superior physical strength, and this control in various forms . . . has continued to the present. As minors, though not to the same extent, she has been looked upon in the courts as needing especial care that her rights may be preserved . . . .it is still true that in the struggle for subsistence she is not an equal competitor with her brother. Though limitations upon personal and contractual rights may be removed by legislation there is that in her disposition and habits of life which will operate against a full assertion of those rights.
>
> . . . *she is so constituted that she will rest upon and look to [man] for protection; that her physical structure and a proper discharge of her maternal functions—having in view not merely her own health, but the well-being of the race—justify legislation to protect her from the greed as well as the passion of man.* The limitations which this statute places upon her contractual powers, upon her right to agree with her employer as to the time she shall labor, are not imposed solely for her benefit, but also largely *for the benefit of all.**

In light of this crudely patronizing statement, it is evident that *Muller* v. *Oregon* is doubly significant. First, the case demonstrates, of course, that as long ago as 1908 the High Court sanctioned state legislation which interfered not only with a businessman's right to run his business his own way, but with a female worker's right to labor each day as long as she wished. Second, and much more important, *Muller* reveals about as nakedly as any case could the *explicit* anti-

---

* *Muller* v. *Oregon*, 208 U.S. 412, 421-423, 28 S.Ct. 324, 326-327 (1908); emphasis added.

individual rights premise from which that decision flowed. To hold women's "physical well-being" and their production of "vigorous offspring" to be matters of "public interest," "in order to preserve the strength and vigor of the race," is to consider women as a mere resource—important to society for their procreational capacity, and to be nurtured much like livestock, and for the same reason. Unfortunately, this view of women was not an aberration confined to *Muller* v. *Oregon*.

In 1913 the State of Washington enacted a minimum wage law applicable only to female workers; men were left free to bargain as they pleased, and to get what they could. Eventually, the statute's constitutionality was challenged, and the *Parrish* case went to the Supreme Court of the United States where the law was upheld.[2]

The Court relied heavily on *Muller* v. *Oregon* to justify the state's control over how much money Washington employers had to pay their female workers. *Parrish* also tracked *Muller's* dangerous view that women's health was of importance to society. Indeed, Chief Justice Hughes's opinion for the Court's majority asked rhetorically: "What can be closer to the public interest than the health of women and their protection from unscrupulous and overreaching employers?" Answering his own question, Hughes explained: "And if the protection of women is a legitimate end of the exercise of state power, how can it be said that the requirement of the payment of a minimum wage fairly fixed in order *to meet the very necessities of existence* is not an admissible means to that end?"* With this emphasis on the female workers' *need* the Court had made explicit something that had only been implicit in *Muller*: because women were a societal resource, government had the power to determine their needs and to compel the satisfaction of those needs by their employers.

Muller and *Parrish* were, of course, *state* cases, and they illustrated the extent to which government even then could control business at that nonfederal level of our two-tiered political system. The other tier of our system is the federal level, and this is an appropriate point at which to explain how the two are constitutionally supposed to coexist and share power.

---

* *West Coast Hotel Co.* v. *Parrish*, 300 U.S. 379, 398, 57 S.Ct. 578, 585 (1937); emphasis added.

The people of America, in the Constitution of the United States, created a new federal government by delegating to it a wide variety of specific powers, especially to Congress. For example, it was given the power to declare war, borrow money, establish post offices, raise and support armies, organize courts, and, as we shall see in a moment, "to regulate commerce . . . among the several states." Because at the time the Constitution was adopted the states feared that its delegation of power to the federal government could be understood to diminish the states' own powers, the Tenth Amendment was added. It provided that: "The powers not delegated to the [federal government] by the Constitution, nor prohibited by it to the States, are reserved to the States respectively, or to the people." In other words, when the federal Constitution was adopted, the states retained all their own powers— except if, in the Constitution itself, a power were specifically given to the federal government or specifically denied to the states.

This two-tier division of power has meant that everyone in the United States is subject, in different aspects of their lives, to both federal and state authority.

Needless to say, the states have not been alone in fully exercising that authority, especially over business activities.

Back in the late 1930s, an Ohio dairy and poultry farmer named Filburn also raised a little winter wheat. Some he would sell, some he would feed to his animals, some he would mill into flour for his own consumption, and the rest he would keep for the next year's seeding.

As part of Franklin Delano Roosevelt's "New Deal," in 1938 the Agricultural Adjustment Act was passed in an attempt, among other things, to support farm prices by controlling the amount of farm production. Each year the bureaucrats figured out how much wheat would be needed the next year, and in 1940, under the authority of the Act, the government told Filburn that for his 1941 wheat crop he could plant no more than eleven acres and harvest no more than about twenty bushels per acre. Ignoring Washington's directive, Filburn sowed and harvested an extra twelve acres. When the government assessed a penalty against him, Filburn refused to pay it, making a very interesting constitutional argument.

Filburn conceded that the federal Constitution *had* vested Congress with the power to regulate interstate commerce, and that just recently the Supreme Court *had* upheld a federal law regulating the local production of goods simply because *later* they went into interstate commerce.[3] But, said Filburn, the Agricultural Adjustment Act was quite different. It went beyond other federal laws, extending federal interstate commerce power to local farm production intended wholly for local consumption and not in any way intended for interstate commerce. How, asked Filburn, could Congress use its interstate commerce power to regulate wheat which would never leave his farm? Not a bad question, and one that deserved a better answer than Filburn received—especially since the wider issue—federal interstate commerce clause regulation of business—was considerably more important than Filburn's few bushels of extra wheat.

To save the Agricultural Adjustment Act, to assure that the federal government could use the interstate commerce clause to control even local business activities if it wished, and to justify its regulation of the locally grown, Filburn-consumed wheat, the Court somehow had to connect that wheat to interstate commerce. Here is how it tried:

> One of the primary purposes of the Act . . . was to increase the market price of wheat and to that end to limit the volume thereof that could affect the market. It can hardly be denied that a factor of such volume and variability as home-consumed wheat would have a substantial influence on price and market conditions. This may arise because being in marketable condition such wheat overhangs the market and if induced by rising prices tends to flow into the market and check price increases. But if we assume that it is never marketed, it supplies a need of the man who grew it which would otherwise be reflected by purchases in the open market. Home-grown wheat in this sense competes with wheat in commerce. The stimulation of commerce is a use of the regulatory function quite as definitely as prohibitions or restrictions thereon.[4]

In other words, regular wheat farmers were hurting from low prices, which could be kept high if wheat production was limited; wheat production had been limited when Congress enacted the A.A.A., pursuant to its interstate commerce power; that regulatory power extended even to Filburn because no matter what he did with his wheat it *would* affect interstate commerce: if he sold his wheat, it would be *in* interstate commerce; if he kept it, he would have no need to buy other wheat that *was* in interstate commerce. Either way, according to the Court, Filburn's wheat had a sufficient connection to interstate commerce to warrant *federal* control of his *local* agricultural production.

Not surprisingly, it is this aspect of *Wickard* v. *Filburn*—concerning the scope of federal interstate commerce power, and the application of that power—which has gotten the most notoriety. Yet even more important about the Court's unanimous opinion in *Wickard* is the unusually explicit altruist-collectivist-statist premise upon which that decision was based. It arose in the Court's response to Filburn's argument that by forcing him and other dairy/poultry farmers into the market to buy small quantities of personally needed wheat which they could easily grow themselves, the Agricultural Adjustment Act and its price support system hurt *them* in order to benefit *regular* wheat farmers. Filburn wanted to know why dairy/poultry farmers should be penalized in order to keep prices high for wheat farmers—another good question, which the Supreme Court answered quite candidly: "It is of the essence of regulation that it lays a restraining hand on the self-interest of the regulated and that advantages from the regulation commonly fall to others."[5]

Self-interest, the Court asserted, was to be restrained, regulated, controlled by government, in favor of the interests of *others*. Filburn's interest in growing a little wheat for his own use was to be subordinated to the need of wheat farmers to obtain a government-supported price higher than the free market would otherwise provide them.

So, just as Oregon and Washington had enacted state laws to subordinate the rights of employers to the government-perceived needs of their female workers, Congress had enacted a federal statute sacrificing the rights of one kind of farmer to the needs of another.

Unfortunately, however, *Wickard* was only an early example of Congress's use of its interstate commerce power to control private business activities on behalf of others thought by the legislature to need government help. For the next fifty years the interstate commerce clause was used to justify government control of transportation, communication, investments, banking, labor relations, power, energy, trade, food and drugs, and much more. Exactly how *much* more is illustrated by a clutch of cases from the sixties and seventies which, for the same reasons that we have already seen, extended federal control even into privately owned local retail establishments.

The Heart of Atlanta Motel had 216 rooms available to transient guests. Accessible to two interstate and two Georgia highways, it solicited business by advertising nationally and by using over fifty billboards and highway signs within the state. The motel accepted convention trade from outside Georgia and about seventy-five percent of its registered guests were from outside the state.

Ollie's Barbecue was a family-owned restaurant in Birmingham, Alabama, catering to a family and white-collar trade and specializing in barbecued meats and homemade pies. It had a seating capacity of 220 and was located on a state highway eleven blocks from an interstate. Bus stations and a railroad were not far away. Ollie's Barbecue purchased about half of its food from a local supplier who, in turn, procured it from outside of Alabama.

Both Heart of Atlanta Motel and Ollie's Barbecue had inflexible policies against accommodating Negroes, the owners of the establishments holding that since the businesses belonged to them, they would serve whom they pleased.

Needless to say, to a great many people in the United States racial discrimination had always—rightly—been anathema, both on the public level, where one found such legislation as the South's "Jim Crow" laws, and in the private sector as well, where it was not uncommon to encounter attitudes like those of the Heart of Atlanta Motel and Ollie's Barbecue. Following World War II, however, gains began to be made against official state and local racial discrimination, and the Supreme Court's landmark public school desegregation case was probably the most striking example from the decade after the War.[6]

The cutting edge in those days in the fight against *official* racial discrimination was the Fourteenth Amendment to the Constitution of the United States, which provides that: " . . . nor shall any *State* deprive any person of life, liberty, or property without due process of law; nor deny to any person within its jurisdiction the equal protection of the laws."* But, for the many who mistakenly erased the critical

---

* Emphasis added.

distinction between public and private conduct, it was not enough to attack merely *public* racial discrimination. They also insisted on reaching the *private* discrimination practiced by all the Heart of Atlanta Motels and Ollie's Barbecues of this country.

This public-private distinction is one which must be carefully understood, especially in regard to racial discrimination. It is axiomatic that *government*—state and federal—must not discriminate, since it is *everyone's* government: Negroes, Caucasians, men, women, young, old, rich, poor. Moreover, the Constitution explicitly prohibits *public* racial discrimination.

On the other hand, as irrational and immoral as *private* racial discrimination is—treating an entire race as an undifferentiated collective whole—the Constitution does not bar it. No more than it bars marrying elderly spinsters for their money, parental indifference to the spiritual needs of their children, or religious bigotry. Indeed, the very nature of a free country and of its Constitution *necessarily* distinguishes between public and private morality.

As much as victims of racial discrimination had a *constitutional* right to nondiscriminatory treatment by *government*, and a *moral* right to it by other *individuals*, these were two entirely separate kinds of rights. To attempt a combination of the two, to assert that the Constitution required private individuals to eschew racial prejudice was, in effect, to make government the arbiter of private morality. It was also to erase the difference between public and private conduct, to compel some people to fulfill the aspirations of others (however legitimate), and, in so doing, to ignore the fact that no one can have their supposed "rights" vindicated by violating the actual rights of others. But none of these points, or any others, prevented the antidiscrimination forces from attempting to convert their moral rights into constitutional ones.

Since the antidiscrimination forces could not use the Fourteenth Amendment for that purpose—because of its requirement that the discriminatory action be taken by the *State*—they went shopping elsewhere. As a result, in the early sixties a broadbased federal Civil Rights Act was proposed, designed to rest on an entirely different base from the Fourteenth Amendment. One part of the Act was intended to reach *private* racially discriminatory conduct in a host of so-called "public accommodations."

Though the proposed legislation had a great many Congressional supporters, some of them, as well as others in the legislature, had serious reservations about whether *Congress* could reach the *private* racially discriminatory practices of local business establishments. The Senate Hearings in 1963 spotlighted the problem:[7]

> Attorney General Kennedy: We base this on the commerce clause.
>
> Senator Moroney: ... many of us are worried about the use the interstate commerce clause will have on matters which have been for more than 170 years thought to be within the realm of local control under our dual system of State and Federal government.
>
> * * *
>
> Senator Moroney: I strongly doubt that we can stretch the interstate commerce clause that far . . . .
>
> * * *
>
> Senator Moroney: If the court decisions . . . mean that a business, no matter how intrastate in its nature, comes under the interstate commerce clause, then we can legislate for other businesses in other fields in addition to the discrimination legislation that is asked for here.
>
> Attorney General Kennedy: If the establishment is covered by the commerce clause, then you can regulate; that is correct . . . .
>
> Senator Thurmond: Mr. Attorney General, isn't it true that all of the acts of Congress based on the commerce clause . . . were primarily designed to regulate economic affairs of life and that the basic purpose of this bill is to regulate moral and social affairs?
>
> Attorney General Kennedy: . . . I think that the discrimination that is taking place at the present time is having a very adverse effect on our economy.

Members of Congress were not the only ones deeply concerned about extending federal interstate commerce power so as to control local business establishments. One of America's most distinguished constitutional law authorities, Professor Gerald Gunther, unequivocally informed the Department of Justice that use of the interstate commerce clause to bar *private* racial discrimination in *local* places of "public accommodation" would be unconstitutional:

> The commerce clause "hook" has been put to some rather strained uses in the past, I know; but the substantive content of the commerce clause would have to be drained beyond any point yet reached to justify

the simplistic argument that all intrastate activity may be subjected to any kind of national regulation merely because some formal crossing of an interstate boundary once took place . . . . The aim of the proposed antidiscrimination legislation, I take it, is quite unrelated to any concern with national commerce in any substantive sense.

It would, I think, pervert the meaning and purpose of the commerce clause to invoke it as the basis for this legislation.[8]

It should be noted that neither the Senators quoted above, nor Professor Gunther, objected to the Civil Rights Act *per se* and the *effect* it would have on private racial discrimination in local business establishments. Indeed, they welcomed both. Their opposition was limited solely to the constitutional base the legislation would rest on, preferring, not the commerce clause, but the Fourteenth Amendment. But the Civil Rights Act of 1964 was enacted anyhow, predicated on Congress's interstate commerce power.[9] Before the end of that year, the constitutionality of its "public accommodations" provisions was before the Supreme Court in the *Heart of Atlanta*[10] and Ollie's Barbecue[11] cases.

The question for the Court in each case was the same: did Congress exceed its constitutional powers under the interstate commerce clause in compelling the owners of local, privately owned businesses to serve customers whom they declined to serve for racially motivated reasons?

The answer was a unanimous, resounding "no".

To reach that result, the Court relied on earlier cases in which it had allowed Congress to regulate such aspects of business as the sale of products, wages and hours, labor relations, crop control, pricing, and more, because those aspects had some connection with interstate commerce. These precedents, together with the motel's and restaurant's tenuous relationship with interstate commerce through the former's guests and the latter's food purchases, were deemed sufficient by the Court to allow Congress to impose the public accommodations provisions of the federal Civil Rights Act on the two local businesses. That conclusion was undesirable for two reasons: as an unwarranted extension of the interstate commerce clause, and as the conversion of legitimate private aspirations into legal entitlements. Even worse, the government's control of business practices once again rested on the premise of subordinating individual rights to the needs of others, as those needs had been perceived by the eyes of government. After all, what had really caused the enactment of the federal Civil Rights Act of 1964? For the revealing answer, let us return to the Senate Hearings quoted above:

> Attorney General Kennedy: Senator, I think that there is an *injustice* that needs to be remedied. We have to find the tools with which to remedy that injustice . . . .
>
> * * *
>
> Senator Cooper: I do not suppose that anyone would seriously contend that the administration is proposing legislation, or the Congress is considering legislation, because it has suddenly determined, after all these years, that segregation is a burden on interstate commerce. We are considering legislation because we believe, as the great majority of people in our country believe, that all citizens have an equal right to have access to goods, services, and facilities which are held out to be available for public use and patronage.
>
> * * *
>
> Senator Pastore: I believe in this bill because I believe in the *dignity of man*, not because it impedes our commerce. I don't think any man has the right to say to another man, you can't eat in my restaurant because you have a dark skin; no matter how clean you are, you can't eat in my restaurant. That deprives a man of his full stature as an American citizen. That shocks me. That hurts me. And that is the reason why I want to vote for this law.
>
> Now it might well be that I can effect the same remedy through the commerce clause. But I like to feel that what we are talking about is *a moral issue, an issue that involves the morality of this great country of ours*.*

In the same vein, the Report of the Senate Commerce Committee had candidly admitted that:

> The primary purpose of * * * [the Civil Rights Act], then, is to solve this problem, the deprivation of personal dignity that surely accompanies denials of equal access to public [sic] establishments. Discrimination is not simply dollars and cents, hamburgers and

---

* Hearings Before the Senate Committee on Commerce on S. 1732, 88th Cong., 1st Sess., parts 1 and 2; emphasis added.

movies; it is the humiliation, frustration and embarrassment that a person must surely feel when he is told that he is unacceptable as a member of the public because of his race or color.[12]

In sum, as Justice Arthur J. Goldberg so clearly admitted when concurring in *Heart of Atlanta* and *Katzenbach*: "The primary purpose of the Civil Rights Act of 1964, however, as the Court recognizes, and as I would underscore, is *the vindication of human dignity* and not mere economics."*

Since the three branches of American government—legislative, executive and judicial—had done just that, though at considerable expense to the motel's and restaurant's owners' individual right to use their own property as they saw fit, what, then, were the net results of *Heart of Atlanta* and *Katzenbach?* Basically, threefold. First, federal regulation of business had taken another giant step forward, through a wholly unjustifiable and constitutionally indefensible extension of Congress's interstate commerce power. Second, the fundamental distinction between public and private conduct, embodied in the Constitution generally and in the Fourteenth Amendment's "state action" requirement in particular, had been virtually erased. Third, as a basic tenet of American constitutional law, once again the premise had been approved that, *in the name of its view of morality*, government possessed the power to violate individual rights and to subordinate them to the needs of others.

To many, the *Heart of Atlanta* and *Katzenbach* decisions seemed to open the door to greatly increased federal regulation of business through the guise of allegedly protecting civil rights. Their fears were not unfounded.

Certain *private* schools in Virginia discriminated racially among applicants, declining to accept Negroes. Children who were excluded, sued. They invoked both the public accommodations sections of the Civil Rights Act of 1964 which had been upheld in *Heart of Atlanta* and *Katzenbach* a decade earlier, and also another, older federal civil rights statute. Apparently deciding that the local private schools were

---

* *Heart of Atlanta Motel, Inc. v. United States*, 379 U.S. 241, 291, 85 S.Ct. 348, 375 (1964); emphasis added.

measurably different from a motel and a restaurant, the children's attorneys withdrew their public accommodations claim before trial, relying only on the older statute, Title 42 U.S.C. Section 1981, which provides that:

> All persons within the jurisdiction of the United States shall have the same right in every State and Territory to make and enforce contracts, to sue, be parties, give evidence, and to the full and equal benefit of all laws and proceedings for the security of persons and property as is enjoyed by white citizens . . . .

Based on this statute, the unsuccessful applicants argued that the private schools could not refuse to make contracts with them solely because they were Negroes. The Supreme Court agreed, holding that Section 1981 did reach purely *private* racial discrimination and that it prohibited *all* racially motivated contract decisions.[13] The implications of the *Runyon* decision were, of course, potentially so scary that two of the majority justices felt obliged virtually to admit that what they were deciding was wrong, and then to explain why they were going along with the majority anyhow.

Justice Powell frankly admitted that "[if] the slate were clean I might well be inclined to agree with [the dissent] that § 1981 was not intended [by the Congress that enacted it in the post-Civil War period] to restrict private contractual choices."[14]

Why the slate was not clean was explained by the other separately concurring justice, John Stevens: not long before, the Court had ruled on some cases which, though perhaps wrongly decided, compelled the result that the majority had reached in *Runyon*. Although Stevens cogently stated why the majority was dead wrong, he went right along with it anyhow. He expressed his willingness quite straightforwardly: even if a century earlier Section 1981 had not been intended by its framers to mean what the *Runyon* majority now interpreted it to mean, no matter, because "it surely accords with the prevailing sense of justice today."[15] Justice Stevens was obviously making two fascinating admissions: on the one hand, he entertained grave reservations about allowing federal civil rights legislation to control the myriad contractual aspects of an individual's business relations; but on the other, he was willing to go along because the country's mood (and/or his own) was less concerned with the right of individuals to run their own businesses their own way, than with the legitimate aspirations of Negroes to enter the American mainstream. Once again, the rights of some had been subordinated to the needs of others by government's exercise of raw power. Once again, when the Court came to the crossroads, it followed the statist path. Since *Heart of Atlanta* and *Katzenbach* meant that the owner of any business deemed to be a "public accommodation" had no right to serve only those customers he or she chose, and since *Runyon* meant that no business could make a racially motivated contract decision, some people speculated about what the Court would do if Congress went so far as actually to impose some sort of racial quotas on business. Those who wondered did not have long to wait.

Several years ago Congress enacted the Public Works Employment Act of 1977,[16] authorizing some $4 billion in federal grants to state and local governments for use in public works projects. There was nothing unusual about that. But one section of the Act[17] *was* extremely unusual. The "minority business enterprise" provision required that at least ten percent of each grant go to contractors who were members of statutorily defined minorities: "Negroes, Spanish-speaking, Orientals, Indians, Eskimos, and Aleuts."

Despite America's unfortunate experience with government racial classifications, despite our constitutional requirements that government be color-blind, despite consistent constitutional interpretations that racial equality was a two-way street protecting our Caucasian majority as well as our various minorities, despite the Public Works Employment Act's unequivocal intent to aid certain minorities and to disadvantage nonminorities solely for racial reasons, a divided Supreme Court upheld the minority business enterprise provision of the Act.

That Congress had enacted and the Court had upheld a provision regulating the flow of sizable public works funds to the construction industry on a strictly racial quota basis is, as usual, not nearly as important as *why* it did so. For the answer, the place to begin is in Congress.

The provision's sponsor had conceded that its objective was to direct funds into the minority business community[18] and "to begin to redress this grievance that has been extant for so long."[19] Another Congressman viewed the provision as promoting "economic equality" and countering a perpetuation of "the historic practices that have precluded minority businesses from effective participation in public contracting opportunities."[20] These attitudes were representative of the thinking of other Members of Congress, though not all, and of the philosophy of earlier business-related programs which had been concerned with helping "racially disadvantaged" businesses.

When the minority business enterprise provision reached the Supreme Court, the question to be decided was whether Congress could constitutionally favor some businesses and disfavor others solely on the basis of a racial and ethnic criterion.

The answer was "yes," though the Court was badly fragmented: Chief Justice Burger and Justices White and Powell joined in one opinion, Powell wrote one of his own, and Justices Marshall, Brennan and Blackmun joined in yet another, to make the six-man majority; the dissents consisted of an opinion by Justice Stewart for himself and Justice Rehnquist, and an opinion by Justice Stevens.

Burger's approach was largely to defer to Congress's concern for the problem of past racial discrimination generally, and minority participation in government-funded construction projects in particular. He observed that:

> Congress, after due consideration, perceived a pressing need to move forward with new approaches in the continuing effort to achieve the goal of equality of economic opportunity. In this effort, Congress has necessary latitude to try new techniques such as the limited use of racial and ethnic criteria to accomplish *remedial objectives* . . . . That the program may press the outer limits of congressional authority affords no basis for striking it down.*

Burger's passing reference to "remedial objectives" was enlarged somewhat by Powell, who observed that "in our quest to achieve a society free from racial classification, we cannot ignore the claims of those who still suffer from the effects of identifiable discrimination."[21] But it was Marshall who named explicitly what all six majority justices

---

* *Fullilove* v. *Klutznick*, 448 U.S. 453, 490, 100 S.Ct. 2758, 2780 (1980); emphasis added.

were really getting at:

> In my separate opinion in *Bakke* [an earlier racial quota case] . . . I
> recounted the "ingenious and pervasive forms of discrimination against
> the Negro" long condoned under the Constitution and concluded that
> "[t]he position of the Negro today in America is the tragic but inevitable
> consequence of centuries of unequal treatment." I there stated:
>
>> "It is because of a legacy of unequal treatment that we now must permit
>> the institutions of this society to give consideration to race in making
>> decisions about who will hold the positions of influence, affluence, and
>> prestige in America. For far too long, the doors to those positions have been
>> shut to Negroes. If we are ever to become a fully integrated society, one in
>> which the color of a person's skin will not determine the opportunities
>> available to him or her, we must be willing to open those doors . . . Those
>> doors cannot be fully opened without the acceptance of race-conscious
>> remedies. As my Brother Blackmun observed in *Bakke*, '[i]n order to get
>> beyond racism, we must first take account of race. There is no other
>> way.'..."
>
> Congress recognized these realities when it enacted the minority set-
> aside provision at issue in this case. Today, by upholding this race-
> conscious remedy, the Court accords Congress the authority necessary
> to undertake the task of moving our society toward a state of meaningful
> equality of opportunity, not an abstract version of equality in which the
> effects of past discrimination would be forever frozen into our social
> fabric. I applaud this result.[22]

So, according to the *Fullilove* majority at least, two wrongs
apparently *did* make a right. If melting the ice of past wrongful public
racial discrimination sent innocent white businessmen into freezing
water simply because of their color, at least on their way down they
would know that their rights were sacrificed for what the government
believed was the cause of racial equality.

Indeed, though the group perceived by government to be needy
constantly changes (e.g., low-paid laundry workers and hotel maids;
marginal wheat farmers; Negroes excluded from segregated motels,
restaurants and private schools; minority construction companies),
whenever government regulates business, the rights of some (laundry
and hotel owners; dairy/poultry farmers; motel, restaurant and private
school operators; contractors) are always sacrificed. Those who are
concerned with the moribund state of business in America would do

well to understand this. The anti-individual rights principles on the basis of which our government has regulated business, as illustrated by the cases discussed in this chapter, are the antithesis of the principles which are necessary to make business, and employers and employees alike, prosper.

2.

PROPERTY *

Any thoughtful observation of history will reveal that, where private-property rights have not been respected and protected, there has not been what we call "human rights."

—*Charles Whittaker,*
Associate Justice,
Supreme Court of the
United States

One infallible barometer of how much freedom there is in a country is the extent to which its citizens control their own property, be it one-family houses, condominiums, farms, raw land, commercial buildings, industrial plants, shopping centers, etc. Unfortunately, in America the barometer has long been falling. The altruist-collectivist ethics, translated into statist political action, has, in effect, completely undercut the right of private property in America, resulting in everything from minor inconveniences to outright uncompensated confiscations.

---

* The concept "property" has a variety of related meanings and usages. It is used here in the sense of a specific piece of land, or of real estate generally.

Fred Sahadi owned the PruneYard Shopping Center in Campbell, California. Five of PruneYard's twenty-one acres were devoted to parking, the balance to walkways, sidewalks, plazas, and buildings containing about sixty-five specialty shops, ten restaurants, and a movie theater. The shopping center had, and nondiscriminatorily enforced, a policy prohibiting both tenants and visitors from engaging in any publicly expressive activity not directly related to PruneYard's commercial purposes, including the circulation of petitions. In other words, PruneYard Shopping Center belonged to Sahadi, and he wanted it used only for shopping.

One Saturday afternoon a group of high school students appeared at the shopping center and set up a card table in a corner of its central courtyard. They began to distribute pamphlets and to request passersby to sign petitions intended for the President and members of Congress, expressing opposition to some United Nations resolution. Soon after, a PruneYard guard informed them of the shopping center's regulations, asked them to leave the private property, and suggested that they relocate to the public sidewalk at PruneYard's perimeter. The students left, but ignored the suggestion. Instead, they sued in the California Superior Court.

The legal action brought by the students was not very complicated: they simply asked the court to compel Mr. Sahadi to allow them access to *his* shopping center, because they wished to distribute their pamphlets and circulate their petitions there.

The trial court denied the students' request, but its decision was no real victory for Mr. Sahadi or for private property: in emphasizing that the students had other adequate and effective means to communicate with their audience, the court's opinion clearly implied that had communication been more difficult for the students, the decision might have been different. The students' appeal to California's intermediate appellate court was equally unsuccessful, and their next stop was the California Supreme Court.

There, the decisions of both lower courts were reversed, the California Supreme Court holding that there was protection for "speech and petitioning, reasonably exercised, in shopping centers even where the centers are privately owned":[1]

It bears repeated emphasis that we do not have under consideration the property or privacy rights of an individual homeowner or the proprietor of a modest retail establishment. As a result of advertising and the lure of a congenial environment, 25,000 persons are induced to congregate daily to take advantage of the numerous amenities offered by the [shopping center] .... A handful of additional orderly persons soliciting signatures and distributing handbills in connection therewith, under reasonable regulations adopted by [the shopping center's owner] to assure that these activities do not interfere with normal business operations ... would not *markedly* dilute [the owner's] property rights.*

Basically, the court was saying: "What the hell, this is a big place with lots of invited people; this expression/petition activity is important to the kids, and it only narrows Sahadi's property rights a little, so we'll let them use his property against his will." However, the *principle* which made the court's conclusion possible was ominous: under certain circumstances—to be evaluated by the courts—individual private property rights *could* be sacrificed to the needs of others.

From the decision of the California Supreme Court, Mr. Sahadi appealed to the Supreme Court of the United States. There, he contended that his constitutional rights had been violated when California allowed his shopping center to be used by people whom he did not want, for purposes of which he disapproved.

The High Court was not sympathetic. Although in an earlier shopping center case, *Lloyd* v. *Tanner*, that Tribunal had encouragingly observed in passing that "property does not 'lose its private character merely because the public is generally invited to use it for designated purposes,' and that '[t]he essentially private character of a store and its privately owned abutting property does not change by virtue of being large or clustered with other stores in a modern shopping center,' "[2] the actual decision in *Lloyd* was considerably more limited. *Lloyd* had held *only* that when a shopping center made its private property available to the public for shopping, the free speech guarantee of the *federal* Constitution did not allow strangers to use the premises for purposes of expression or petitioning. *Lloyd* expressly had left open the question of whether *anything else* might

---

* *Robins* v. *PruneYard Shopping Center*, 23 Cal. 3d 899, 910-911, 153 Cal.Rptr. 854, 860-861, 592 P.2d, 341, 347-348 (1979); emphasis added.

have allowed them to do so. That question was answered in *PruneYard*, where the "anything else" turned out to be the *California* constitution. That constitution, on which the California Supreme Court had based its decision, provided that:

> Every person may freely speak, write and publish his or her sentiments on all subjects, being responsible for the abuse of this right. A law may not restrain or abridge liberty of speech or press.[3]

> * * *

> [P]eople have the right to . . . petition government for redress of grievances.[4]

These familiar provisions were, of course, comparable to the freedom of speech, press and petition guarantees found in all other state constitutions and in the Constitution of the United States. Their intention everywhere was thought to be clear: to protect the individual's right of expression, certainly not to invade another individual's private property. Few would have believed, for example, that in the name of free press a would-be publisher could use *The New York Times*'s printing equipment against its will. Yet, in principle, that is exactly what the California Supreme Court had done in *PruneYard*. It had decided that the free speech and petition provisions of its constitution not only gave the students the right to distribute pamphlets and obtain signatures on their petitions (which no one could legitimately quarrel with), but to do so on Mr. Sahadi's private property. Although California's interpretation/application of free expression was surely perverse, the Supreme Court of the United States nevertheless went along with it. Distinguishing *Lloyd* v. *Tanner* from *PruneYard*, the High Court concluded that in *Lloyd* "there was no *state* constitutional or statutory provision that had been construed to create rights to the use of private property by strangers, comparable to those found to exist by the California Supreme Court here."*

So the Court's previous tough talk in *Lloyd* v. *Tanner*—that private

---

* *PruneYard Shopping Center* v. *Robins*, 447 U.S. 74, 81, 100 S.Ct. 2035, 2040 (1980); emphasis added.

property open to the public did not thereby become public property—really contained a crucial, though implicit, "unless": a shopping center would remain private property *unless* the state in which it was located created, by constitution or statute, "rights" in that center for strangers. Since California's constitution (as construed) had done just that, the Supreme Court of the United States was satisfied. The implications of *PruneYard* are far-reaching: since every state in America has free speech, press, and petition guarantees in *its* constitution, if those guarantees are interpreted to create ersatz rights while destroying genuine rights, the Supreme Court will not object. Indeed, the Court has already told us so, admitting quite explicitly to the need-over-rights premise that motivated its decision in *PruneYard* and which would affect future decisions involving private property:

> [N]either property rights nor contract rights are absolute . . . .
> Equally fundamental with the private right is that of the public to
> regulate it in the common interest . . . .[5]

The altruist-collectivist ethics that made possible *PruneYard*'s statist violation of Mr. Sahadi's private property rights have infected other aspects of ownership as well. For example, it is popularly supposed that today, despite extensive government control of private property, it is still possible to sell one's own property (or not) to whomever one wishes. Unfortunately, that supposition is quite mistaken.

Following the Civil War, Congress enacted the Civil Rights Act of 1866. One of its provisions evolved into the following federal statute:

> All citizens of the United States shall have the same right, in every
> State and Territory, as is enjoyed by white citizens thereof to inherit,
> purchase, lease, sell, hold and convey real and personal property.[6]

When, in the mid-1960s, a white developer in St. Louis refused to sell a house to a Negro named Jones, he sued under Section 1982. Although it had long been the law—rightly—that *government* could not discriminatorily deny any American the right to buy or rent property because of race or color, neither Section 1982 nor any other provision of law had ever been held applicable to purely *private* racial discrimination in housing. So the question that the Supreme Court eventually had to decide in *Jones* v. *Alfred H. Mayer Co.*⁷ was obviously an important one.

In a seven-to-two majority opinion written by Justice Stewart, which relied very heavily on what had been the original intent of Congress when it enacted the statute, the Supreme Court held that Section 1982 prohibited *"all* discrimination against Negroes in the sale or rental of property—discrimination by private owners as well as discrimination by public authorities."*

The Court's conclusion also rested in part on the Thirteenth Amendment, which had abolished slavery. Justice Stewart wrote that:

> Negro citizens, North and South, who saw in the Thirteenth Amendment a promise of freedom—freedom to "go and come at pleasure" [footnote omitted] and to "buy and sell when they please" [footnote omitted]—would be left with "a mere paper guarantee" [footnote omitted] if Congress were powerless to assure that a dollar in the hands of a Negro will purchase the same thing as a dollar in the hands of a white man. At the very least, the freedom that Congress is empowered to secure under the Thirteenth Amendment includes the freedom to buy whatever a white man can buy, the right to live wherever a white man can live."⁸

There were two shortcomings in the majority's approach. One, ably dealt with in Justice Harlan's dissent (joined by Justice White) was that neither the language of the statute itself, nor the Congressional intent on which the majority had predicated its interpretation of the statute, was nearly so supportive of the majority's conclusion as Justice Stewart contended. Justice Harlan put the point nicely when he noted that:

> [My] analysis of the language, structure, and legislative history of the 1866 Civil Rights Act shows, I believe, that the Court's thesis that the Act was meant to extend to purely private action is open to the most serious doubt, if indeed it does not render that thesis wholly untenable. Another, albeit less tangible, consideration points in the same direc-

---

* *Jones* v. *Alfred H. Mayer Co.*, 392 U.S. 409, 421, 88 S.Ct. 2186, 2194 (1968); emphasis in original.

tion. Many of the legislators who took part in the congressional debates inevitably must have shared the individualistic ethic of their time, which emphasized personal freedom [footnote omitted] and embodied a distaste for governmental interference which was soon to culminate in the era of laissez-faire [footnote omitted]. It seems to me that most of these men would have regarded it as a great intrusion on individual liberty for the government to take from a man the power to refuse for personal reasons to enter into a purely private transaction involving the disposition of property, albeit those personal reasons might reflect racial bias.[9]

Interestingly, although Harlan's analysis led him to disagree with the majority's *conclusion*, he did not disagree with the majority's basic premise that purely private racial discrimination *could* be prohibited by government power. Indeed, between the time of oral argument in *Jones* in April 1968 and the case's decision in June 1968, Congress had enacted the Civil Rights Act of 1968, containing comprehensive "fair housing" provisions dealing with the refusal to sell real property for racial reasons. Harlan considered the entire new Civil Rights Act "presumptively constitutional."[10]

The other shortcoming in the majority's approach was a failure adequately to distinguish between the nature and significance of *private* versus *government* action.* A concurring opinion by Justice Douglas inadvertently highlighted that failure. As usual, he was eloquent but overbroad, glossing over the crucial distinction on which the case, and the principle behind it, rested. Douglas correctly observed that, unfortunately: "Some badges of slavery remain today. While the institution has been outlawed, it has remained in the minds and hearts of many white men. Cases which have come to this Court depict a spectacle of slavery unwilling to die."[11] Then, he listed examples. Without distinguishing between government and private action, he threw into the same undifferentiated pot racially segregated *public* schools, and racially discriminatory *private* restaurants; *state* laws against racial intermarriage, and *personal* racial preferences in renting motel rooms; *municipal* ordinances establishing residential

---

* Although Harlan did discuss that difference in his analysis of the statute's legislative history, he failed to assess its significance.

districts according to race, and *individual* refusals to sell real estate because of racial prejudice.

Douglas's refusal to distinguish between private and government discrimination; and the majority's mistaken willingness to believe that the 1866 Congress intended to prohibit even private racial discrimination in the transfer of real property; and Harlan's disagreement only with the interpretation of the legislative history, but not with the principle that government can bar private racial discrimination in housing; and, finally, enactment of the Civil Rights Act of 1968 with its Fair Housing Title;[12] all compel the conclusion that today a property owner *cannot* refuse to sell because of racially discriminatory motives. By implication, any discrimination on grounds of religion, alienage, national origin, and even gender is probably also not allowed. All these prohibitions, of course, are in the name of ethics— specifically those of the majority, which apparently has no qualms about subordinating to its own values those of the property owner.

We know from *PruneYard* that through perverse interpretations of state free speech, press and petition guarantees, government possesses the power to open up private property to the use of strangers. We know from *Jones* that government has the power to control transfers of private property through so-called civil rights laws. Clearly, the weight of government on the private property owner grows heavier still. But even these powers do not tell the complete story. To them must be added another formidable government power: controlling how the owner of private property may actually *use* it.

The granddaddy of Supreme Court land-use cases is *Euclid* v. *Ambler Realty Co.*[13] Ambler owned sixty-eight acres in the village of Euclid, Ohio. In 1922 the village enacted a comprehensive zoning ordinance which had a substantial impact on Ambler's property. As the Supreme Court said:

> . . . the tract of land in question is vacant and has been held for years for the purpose of selling and developing it for industrial uses, for which it is especially adapted, being immediately in the path of progressive industrial development; that for such uses it has a market value of about $10,000 per acre, but if the use be limited to residential purposes the market value is not in excess of $2,500 per acre; that the first 200 feet of the parcel back from Euclid Avenue, if unrestricted in respect of use,

has a value of $150 per front foot, but if limited to residential uses, and ordinary mercantile business be excluded therefrom, its value is not in excess of $50 per front foot.[14]

Ambler went to court, alleging that severe limitations on how it could use its own land had been unconstitutionally imposed by other people, who held in their hands the coercive legal powers of the village. The Supreme Court disagreed, holding the zoning limitations constitutional. Relying on earlier cases that had upheld less onerous restrictions (e.g., building heights), pointing to the zoning ordinance's alleged usefulness in making life in the residential area more tranquil and pleasant, and recognizing that through the ordinance "a majority of [Euclid's] inhabitants" were merely "voicing their will,"[15] the Court upheld the land-use scheme. The net result was that from then on, the use to which all real property could be put—not just in Euclid, Ohio, but everywhere—would be determined not by its owners, but by whoever held the government's political power.

For the next fifty years that is precisely what happened. Virtually every town, village, city, and county in America has enacted and enforced zoning laws to control every aspect of land use. Nothing has been too great or too small to regulate—from the kinds of activities that could be conducted, to minimum plot sizes, to set-back requirements, and even to the height of T.V. antennas.

Finally, after nearly half a century of tight land-use control, in 1974 the Supreme Court had an opportunity to take another look at zoning.

Belle Terre, a tiny Long Island village of 220 homes not far from a state university, was concerned about student rooming houses. So its zoning ordinance restricted land use to one-family homes. "Family" was defined as: "[o]ne or more persons related by blood, adoption, or marriage, living or cooking together as a single housekeeping unit . . . . A number of persons but not exceeding two . . . living and cooking together as a single housekeeping unit though not related by blood, adoption, or marriage shall be deemed to constitute a family."[16] Because the ordinance barred more than two "unrelated" persons from living together in Belle Terre, the owners of one house and three of their illegal tenants sued the village, mounting a broad-based constitutional attack. They alleged that the ordinance:

. . . interferes with a person's right to travel . . . with the right to migrate to and settle within a State; that it bars people who are uncongenial to the present residents; that it expresses the social preferences of the residents for groups that will be congenial to them; that social homogeneity is not a legitimate interest of government; that the restriction of those whom the neighbors do not like trenches on the newcomers' rights of privacy; that it is of no rightful concern to villagers whether the residents are married or unmarried; that the ordinance is antithetical to the Nation's experience, ideology, and self-perception as an open, egalitarian, and integrated society.[17]

Some of these allegations—"uncongeniality," "social preferences," "social homogeneity"—nicely spotlighted the underlying purpose not only of the Belle Terre ordinance, but of all zoning: to express a collective preference for who shall live (or be in business, or conduct certain activities, etc.) in a given area, and under what conditions.

The Supreme Court's response to the constitutional attack in *Belle Terre* was to invoke the *Euclid* case as a precedent supporting government control of private land use. Just as nearly fifty years earlier the Court had deferred to the village of Euclid's determination that certain "desirable" public purposes would be served by regulating how its landowners could use their own property, the Court similarly deferred to the village of Belle Terre:

. . . boarding houses, fraternity houses, and the like present urban problems. More people occupy a given space; more cars rather continuously pass by; more cars parked; noise travels with crowds.

A quiet place where yards are wide, people few, and motor vehicles restricted are legitimate guidelines in a land-use project addressed to family needs. This goal is a permissible one . . . . The police power is not confined to elimination of filth, stench, and unhealthy places. It is ample to lay out zones where family values, youth values, and the blessings of quiet seclusion and clean air make the area a sanctuary for people.[18]

This statement, the core of the Court's conclusion in *Belle Terre*, is triply significant. For one thing, it reiterated the Court's fifty-year-old approval of the government's power to zone, providing a shot in the arm to proponents of even more stringent land use controls. (We shall see the consequences of that in a few moments.) For another, the *Belle Terre* opinion again clearly revealed that the same old doctrine— altruism-collectivism-statism—underlies government's willingness to subordinate individual interests to the needs of society. Here, the owner's and renters' desire to use the house for a student rooming house was subordinated to community values (e.g., quiet, clean air, etc.). Finally, *Belle Terre* again showed that even though individual justices may disagree about the *outcome* of a particular case, they all hold the same basic premises and any disagreement is only on the facts and/or their application, not on the *principle*.

In this regard, it is fascinating to contrast Justice Douglas's* majority opinion with that of his colleague Justice Marshall. Since Douglas had upheld the ordinance because he believed in zoning, one might be tempted to think that since Marshall dissented, he opposed zoning. Not so. Once again, all sides of a case agreed on the *principle*, though perhaps not on its specific application. Indeed, Marshall began his dissent by proudly stating that:

> I am in full agreement with the majority that zoning is a complex and important function of the State. It may indeed be the most essential function performed by local government, for it is one of the primary means by which we protect that sometimes difficult to define concept of quality of life. I therefore continue to adhere to the principle of *Village of Euclid* v. *Ambler Realty Co.* . . . , that deference should be given to governmental judgments concerning proper land-use allocation.
>
> * * *
>
> I would also agree with the majority that local zoning authorities may properly act in furtherance of the objectives asserted to be served by the ordinance at issue here: restricting uncontrolled growth, solving traffic problems, keeping rental costs at a reasonable level, and making the community attractive to families.†

---

* Yes, indeed—the *Belle Terre* Court's opinion upholding the ultra-restrictive, exclusionary zoning ordinance was authored by the Court's arch-liberal. Douglas classified the issue in *Belle Terre* not as one involving "individual rights," but only "property rights," thus making *Belle Terre* another prime example of the futility of trying to distinguish between rights.

† *Village of Belle Terre* v. *Boraas*, 416 U.S. 1, 13, 94 S.Ct. 1536, 1543 (1974). Marshall's dissent was predicated on the belief, not shared by any of the other eight justices, that though zoning ordinances were generally constitutional, Belle Terre's law violated constitutional rights of "association" and "privacy."

With virtually all the justices agreeing on a principle which results in decisions like *Euclid* and *Belle Terre*, it is obvious that the land-use rights of private property owners are virtually nonexistent. Indeed, that principle and those cases were the basis for one of the Court's most recent zoning decisions, *Agins* v. *City of Tiburon*[19]—a case which shows dramatically just how far government's zoning power really extends, and which suggests that land-use control may even reach beyond zoning.

Land in Tiburon, California, is reputed to be the most expensive suburban property in the entire state. Agins and others bought five acres of unimproved land there for residential development, ridgelands possessing magnificent views of San Francisco Bay and the scenic surrounding area, property among the best in Tiburon.

After the purchase had been made, California required Tiburon (and other municipalities) to prepare a general plan governing both land use and the development of open space land. So Tiburon adopted two ordinances, finding that:

> [i]t is in the public interest to avoid unnecessary conversion of open space land to strictly urban uses, thereby protecting against the resultant adverse impacts, such as air, noise and water pollution, traffic congestion, destruction of scenic beauty, disturbance of the ecology and the environment, hazards related to geology, fire and flood, and other demonstrated consequences of urban sprawl.[20]

The ordinances significantly altered the zoning which had been in place when Agins and his associates bought the property, and basically created one-acre zoning that limited the development of Agins's five-acre parcel to no more than five single-family dwellings. But that was not the end of it. No construction would be allowed until the builder's plan had been deemed compatible with adjoining patterns of development and open space. In evaluating that plan, the city would have to consider how well the proposed development would preserve the surrounding environment and whether the new construction's density would be offset by adjoining open spaces.

Needless to say, a lawsuit ensued. The landowners contended that changing the zoning *after* they bought (but before they built), and making the new zoning so restrictive, violated their constitutional rights. So much so, they argued, as to constitute an actual governmental "taking" of their property. After losing in the California courts, the owners reached the Supreme Court. They should have stayed home.

Relying on *Euclid* and *Belle Terre*, the Court held that "the zoning ordinances substantially advance legitimate governmental goals. The State of California has determined that the development of local open-space plans will discourage the 'premature and unnecessary conversion of open-space land to urban use'....[These]...zoning regulations...are exercises of the city's police power to protect the residents of Tiburon from the ill-effects of urbanization."[21] Accordingly, the aesthetic values of the majority prevailed, the zoning ordinances were held unconstitutional, and there had been no illegal "taking."

This concept of "taking" arose in *Agins* because of a Constitutional mandate limiting, at least to a slight extent, what government can do to private property. The Fifth Amendment to the United States Constitution provides among other things, that no "private property [shall] be taken for public use, without just compensation." This "eminent domain clause" is both a grant of power authorizing government to take private property for public use, and somewhat of a limitation on that power because of its requirement that just compensation be paid.

Over the years, government has invoked its power of eminent domain to obtain property for building roads, parks, bridges, reservoirs. Frequently, unhappy property owners have litigated with the government concerning whether the confiscation of their private property was actually for "public use" (e.g., private land condemned by government, but turned over to developers for low cost housing), and whether the payment they were offered was adequate.

As *Agins* illustrates, property owners have also litigated with the government concerning whether its zoning extended so far as to become a *de facto* "taking" in the constitutional sense (requiring the payment of just compensation). Usually, as in *Agins*, the government and its zoning wins. Occasionally, however, they lose, and courts will not allow *zoning* to extend quite so far as the authorities wish. When that happens, and when the government declines to use eminent domain because of the financial cost, the authorities try a different approach.

Beginning in 1927, sand and gravel was mined from a pit located in the Long Island town of Hempstead. Virtually from the start the excavation had reached the water table, resulting in a water-filled crater which over time had been deepened and widened so that by the late 1950s it was a twenty-acre lake, with an average depth of twenty-five feet. The town, of course, had long attempted to regulate mining excavations within its limits. For example, a 1945 ordinance had required that sand and gravel pits be enclosed by a wire fence, and there were shoulder and slope requirements. The pit's owner complied. No matter. The town still tried to prevent further excavation, next contending that the pit violated the town's zoning ordinance. But the New York courts sided with the owner, holding that since he had been mining sand and gravel before the zoning ordinance was adopted he possessed "a prior non-conforming use" and so could not be stopped. At least not by the zoning law.

Undeterred in its efforts to close down the sand and gravel pit, and having failed in its attempt to do so by means of its zoning ordinance, in 1958 the town amended the 1945 ordinance—allegedly not a zoning law, but rather a "safety" regulation. The amendment made the shoulder, slope, and fence requirements tougher, prohibited any excavating below the water table, and imposed on the pit's owner an affirmative duty to refill any excavation below that level. Since the water table had been reached some thirty years earlier in that twenty-acre, twenty-five-foot-deep lake, the amendment of the town's "safety" regulation was tantamount to legislating the sand and gravel pit out of existence. That is clearly what the town intended.

After about a year, during which the owner had, of course, not complied with the amended ordinance, the town sued to stop all further excavation. In response, the pit's owner invoked the Fifth Amendment's eminent domain clause, and argued that the law was unconstitutional principally because "it was not regulatory of their business but completely prohibitory and confiscated [his] property without compensation."[22]

So the issue was presented in bold relief: having failed to control Goldblatt's land use by conventional zoning means, and being unwilling to take his sand and gravel pit under eminent domain (and pay just compensation), could the town instead "regulate" that use out of existence through a so-called safety ordinance? Justice Clark's five-page answer, written for a *unanimous* Supreme Court, was startling indeed.

The Court's opinion began with a candid concession: " . . . the ordinance completely prohibits a beneficial use to which the property has previously been devoted," and a surprising disclaimer that: " . . . such a characterization does not tell us whether or not the ordinance is unconstitutional."[23] In other words, although the town put Goldblatt out of business, by itself that was not enough to make the "safety regulation" unconstitutional. "There is," observed the Court, "no set formula to determine where regulation [or, in other cases, zoning] ends and taking begins," and so "[t]he question, therefore narrows to whether the prohibition of further excavation below the water table is a valid exercise of the town's police power."[24]

In saying this, the Supreme Court was recognizing two discrete categories of government action (apart from zoning, which was something else entirely) to which privately owned real estate was subject: regulation and eminent domain. The former, not involving a taking, would require no compensation. The latter would. Additionally, despite its eschewing a formula, the Court seemed nevertheless to be establishing a test for distinguishing regulation from eminent domain: a valid exercise of "police power" would constitute merely noncompensable regulation, not a taking.

The Court's explanation of what the police power concept meant underscored once again the anti-individual rights premise which has been at the core of government action generally, and of Supreme Court decision making in particular. "The term 'police power,' " said the Court, "connotes the time-tested conceptual limit of public encorachment upon private interests. . . . The classic statement of the rule . . . is still valid today":

> To justify the state in . . . interposing its authority in behalf of the public, it must appear—First, that the interests of the public . . . require such interference; and, second, that the means are reasonably necessary for the accomplishment of the purpose, and not unduly oppressive upon individuals.[25]

This brief quotation, used with approval by the Supreme Court in the 1960s virtually to destroy a use of private property deemed to be unacceptable by the community, was from an *1894* Supreme Court case. In it, the Supreme Court of the United States nakedly yet unashamedly admitted that some individuals can be oppressed (though not "unduly") by government power exercised on behalf of the public (i.e., other people). That 1894 statement demonstrates the tenacity and durability of the altruist-collectivist-statist doctrines that have infected our political-legal system from its beginning.

The application of those doctrines is far wider than government's control over private property, as the next chapter amply demonstrates.

3.

CONTRACTS

... the movement of the progressive societies has hither-
to been a movement from Status to Contract.

— *Henry Sumner Maine*

In our daily lives all of us come into contact with hundreds of other
people: loved ones, fellow workers, casual acquaintances, total
strangers. Some of these many contacts—e.g., being hit by a car, or
mugged—are involuntary. But most relationships between people in
the United States—with spouses, landlords, employers, lawyers,
physicians—are voluntarily chosen.

To the extent that voluntarily chosen relationships create important
obligations—which later may have to be clearly recalled, and perhaps
even legally enforced—it is necessary to create *contracts*. Contracts
are the cement that binds together the voluntary assent of free
individuals. Without contracts, little or nothing would ever be
accomplished, from "buying" dinner at McDonalds (what would you
receive, or pay?) or "renting" an apartment (which one, for how long,
at what cost?) to "building" a home (the many terms in a project even
as relatively simple as this boggle the mind).

Because enforceable private choices are a cornerstone of a free country, and because contracts are indispensable to those choices, the Founding Fathers specifically provided in the Constitution itself that the state governments could enact no "law impairing the obligation of contracts".* In other words, the Constitution forbade government— expressly the states; by implication, the federal government as well— from stepping between the contracting parties and rewriting their agreement either for the government's own purposes, or for anyone else's benefit. Unfortunately, however, even explicit Constitutional safeguards have not been able to protect the sanctity of private choice from government's designs. Four famous Supreme Court cases— involving "legal tender," mortgages, gold clauses, and restrictive land covenants—eloquently answer the question of whether, in America, a contract is really worth the paper it is written on.

In a free, capitalist country contracts involving financial matters are particularly important. Loan contracts, such as consumer credit transactions and corporate borrowing, for example, play a large part in the efficient functioning of a market economy. It is with a financial contract that our story begins.

Prior to the Civil War, the only lawful money in the United States was gold and silver coin. When it was loaned, repayment was expected in kind. Then, early in 1862, in order to finance that extremely costly war, Congress created paper money. These "green-backs" were made "legal tender," which, by law, had to be accepted in payment of debt, regardless of whether the creditor wanted them or how much they were worth. Although loan contracts (in the form of promissory notes) had been expressed by the parties in terms of gold and/or silver coin, by means of the Legal Tender Act the government had rewritten their contracts, forcing paper money of dubious value on creditors to the very great advantage of debtors.

Obviously, the Legal Tender Act's effect on existing loan contracts raised a serious constitutional question—one which was quickly resolved in *Knox* v. *Lee*.[1] In that case *(Legal Tender II)*, the Supreme Court, quite offhandedly, found that the Act had not interfered with the private loan agreement. The Court merely observed that "[e]very

---

* Constitution of the United States of America, Article I, Section 10.

contract for the payment of money, simply, is necessarily subject to the . . . power of the government over the currency, whatever that power may be . . . ."[2] The Court had little more to say, despite the significance of the contract interference claim, and despite the fact that the *Knox* decision created a windfall for debtors at the expense of their creditors.

A fuller explanation of why government legislation would be allowed to rewrite the terms of existing debt contracts would have to wait sixty-three years until the Supreme Court's decision in *Home Building & Loan Ass'n* v. *Blaisdell.*[3]

On August 1, 1928, Mr. and Mrs. John H. Blaisdell sat down with the Home Building & Loan Association and mortgaged a two-story residential building in Minneapolis. A mortgage, of course, is simply a contract in which the owner of property (the "mortgagor") pledges it to a creditor (the "mortgagee") as the security for the payment of a debt. Usually, a mortgage debt arises when the mortgagee lends the mortgagor the money with which to buy the property. A common example is the purchase of a home (involving a realty mortgage) or an automobile (involving a chattel mortgage).

The Blaisdells' mortgage contract with Home Building & Loan contained customary, rather uncomplicated terms. In return for the Blaisdells putting up their property as security, Home Building & Loan advanced them a given sum of money. They agreed to repay it in regular installments, at a specified rate of interest. If they defaulted by failing to make their payments, Home Building & Loan could protect its loan by foreclosing the mortgage, advertising the property for sale, and then selling it. If the sale brought more than what Home Building & Loan was owed, the excess proceeds would go to the Blaisdells; if it brought less, they would owe Home Building & Loan any deficiency. Either way, an implicit term of the mortgage contract was a long-standing Minnesota law providing for a one-year redemption period following a foreclosure sale, during which time the Blaisdells could reacquire the property for the price at which it had been sold. Only if the redemption period expired without the Blaisdells having exercised their statutory right to reacquire the property, would the buyer at the foreclosure sale have clear title to it.

For a few years the Blaisdells made their regular installment payments. Then they stopped. A foreclosure sale followed, and Home Building & Loan "bought" the property for exactly what the Blaisdells then owed on the mortgage. The sale yielded no excess proceeds for the Blaisdells, and no deficiency was owed by them to Home Building & Loan, which now "sort of" owned the property. Since the foreclosure sale had been on May 2, 1932, the Blaisdells ordinarily would have had only until May 2, 1933, to redeem the property from Home Building & Loan. But a few weeks before the expiration of the one-year redemption period, something happened to change the Blaisdells' position. The State of Minnesota, not Home Building & Loan and the Blaisdells, rewrote the mortgage contract.

On April 18, 1933, a mere fourteen days before the redemption period would have expired, the Minnesota Mortgage Moratorium Law was enacted. The reason for the statute's enactment was best expressed by the state legislature:

> Whereas, the severe financial and economic depression existing for several years past has resulted in extremely low prices for the products of the farms and the factories, a great amount of unemployment, an almost complete lack of credit for farmers, business men and property owners and a general and extreme stagnation of business, agriculture and industry, and

> Whereas, many owners of real property, by reason of said conditions, are unable, and it is believed, will for some time be unable to meet all payments as they come due of taxes, interest and principal of mortgages on their properties and are, therefore, threatened with loss of such properties through mortgage foreclosure and judicial sales thereof, and

> Whereas, many such properties have been and are being bid in at mortgage foreclosure . . . sales for prices much below what is believed to be their real values and often for much less than the mortgage . . . indebtedness, thus entailing deficienc[ies] . . . against the mortgage[es] . . . , and

> Whereas, it is believed, and the legislature of Minnesota hereby declares its belief, that the conditions existing . . . has created an emergency of such nature that justifies and validates legislation for the extension of the time of redemption from mortgage foreclosure . . . sales and other relief of a like character, and

> Whereas, The State of Minnesota possesses the right under its police power to declare a state of emergency to exist, and

> Whereas, the inherent and fundamental purpose of our government

is to safeguard the public and promote the general welfare of the people, and

Whereas, Under existing conditions the foreclosure of many real estate mortgages by advertisement would prevent fair, open and competitive bidding . . . , and

Whereas, It is believed, and the Legislature of Minnesota hereby declares its belief, that the conditions existing . . . have created an emergency of such a nature that justifies and validates changes in legislation providing for the temporary manner, method, terms and conditions upon which mortgage foreclosure sales may be had or postponed . . .

* * *

Section 1. *Emergency Declared to Exist.*—In view of the situation . . . the Legislature of the State of Minnesota hereby declares that a public economic emergency does exist in the State of Minnesota.*

In order to implement the state's newly declared policy to aid defaulting mortgagees, the Minnesota Mortgage Moratorium Law provided that foreclosure sales could be postponed and the redemption period extended until as long as May 1, 1935.

For the Blaisdells, who faced a May 2, 1933 redemption cutoff, the April 18, 1933 Moratorium Law was made to order. They asked the state trial court for an order extending the redemption period, but failed to obtain one. Apparently remembering that Article I, Section 10, of the federal Constitution prohibited a state from enacting any "law impairing the obligation of contracts," and apparently grasping that the Minnesota Mortgage Moratorium Law did just that, the court denied the Blaisdells the extension they sought. When they appealed to the Minnesota Supreme Court, however, it was a different story. Reversing the trial court's decision, the Minnesota Supreme Court accommodatingly extended the Blaisdells' redemption period for the limit—all the way to May 1, 1935. (There was one condition: that the Blaisdells pay $40 monthly "rent" to Home Building & Loan.)

Consider the position of Home Building & Loan. Its loan had been defaulted by the Blaisdells. It had to repurchase the property. It had to wait for almost the entire one-year redemption period to expire (so that it would have clear title to the property), only to be thwarted by

---

* *Home Building & Loan Ass'n* v. *Blaisdell*, 290 U.S. 398, 421, 54 S.Ct. 231, 233-234 (1934); emphasis in original.

Minnesota's legislature and its Supreme Court, which presumed to rewrite the mortgage. The net result? Home Building & Loan would have to wait yet another two years before obtaining possession of, let alone being able to sell, its own property. We already know why the state legislature enacted the law. But why did Minnesota's High Court uphold it against a Contract Clause challenge?

> . . . as an emergency measure [the U.S. Supreme Court would later explain]. Although conceding that the obligations of the mortgage contract were impaired, the [Minnesota Supreme Court] decided that what it thus described as an impairment was, notwithstanding the contract clause of the federal Constitution, within the police power of the state as that power was called into exercise by the public economic emergency which the Legislature had found to exist.[4]

The Minnesota Supreme Court was even more explicit about what motivated its decision:

> In addition to the weight to be given to the determination of the Legislature that an economic emergency exists which demands relief, the court must take notice of other considerations. The members of the Legislature come from every community of the state and from all the walks of life. They are familiar with conditions generally in every calling, occupation, profession, and business in the state. Not only they, but the courts must be guided by what is common knowledge. It is common knowledge that in the last few years land values have shrunk enormously. Loans made a few years ago upon the basis of the then going values cannot possibly be replaced on the basis of present values.
>
>   *   *   *
>
> The present nation wide and world wide business and financial crisis has the same results as if it were caused by flood, earthquake, or disturbance in nature. It has deprived millions of persons in this nation of their employment and means of earning a living for themselves and their families; it has destroyed the value of and the income from all property on which thousands of people depended for a living; it actually has resulted in the loss of their homes by a number of our people, and threatens to result in the loss of their homes by many other people in this state; it has resulted in such widespread want and suffering among our people that private, state and municipal agencies are unable to adequately relieve the want and suffering, and Congress has found it

necessary to step in and attempt to remedy the situation by federal aid. Millions of the people's money were and are yet tied up in closed banks and in business enterprises.[5]

In other words, "by common knowledge" things were rough for debtors.

But they were rough for lenders, too, so Home Building & Loan appealed to the Supreme Court of the United States.

Charles Evans Hughes, Chief Justice of the United States, wrote the narrowly divided Court's majority opinion, upholding the constitutionality of the Minnesota law. Though the opinion is lengthy, Hughes conceded that some of what he discussed had no direct bearing on the Minnesota statute before the Court. Much of the balance of his opinion consists of a survey of some of the Court's previous cases, on the basis of which Hughes enunciated a startlingly candid conclusion:

> It is manifest from this review of our decisions that there has been a growing appreciation of public needs and of the necessity of finding ground for a rational *compromise between individual rights and public welfare*. The settlement and consequent contraction of the public domain, the pressure of a constantly increasing density of population, the interrelation of the activities of our people and the complexity of our economic interests, have inevitably led to an increased use of the organization of society in order to protect the very bases of individual opportunity. Where, in earlier days, it was thought that only the concerns of individuals or of classes were involved, and that those of the state itself were touched only remotely, it has later been found that the fundamental interests of the state are directly affected; and that the question is no longer merely that of one party to a contract as against another, but the use of reasonable means to safeguard the economic structure upon which the good of all depends.*

What the Chief Justice was saying could not be any clearer or more consistent with what the Court had done in *Knox* v. *Lee (Legal Tender II)*. Postulating an ever-increasingly complicated social environment in which "the good of all" was the standard of value,

---

* *Home Building & Loan Ass'n* v. *Blaisdell*, 290 U.S. 398, 442, 54 S.Ct. 231, 241 (1938); emphasis added.

Hughes held that "public needs" or "public welfare" or "fundamental interests of the state" had to be protected from something perniciously antithetical: "individual rights." What was necessary, according to Hughes and the Court's majority, was a "rational compromise between individual rights and public welfare."

Since a compromise is "a settlement in which each side gives up some demands or makes concessions,"* the concept can have no application to individual rights, which are either absolute or nonexistent.

Indeed, the majority's idea of a compromise—between the sanctity of contracts supposedly guaranteed in the Constitution's Contract Clause, and the "public welfare" that allegedly required a two-year extension of the redemption period—was to allow Minnesota to rewrite Home Building & Loan's contract with the Blaisdells, profoundly altering one of its most important terms. So much for compromise—and for rights.

Not surprisingly, there was a dissent in *Blaisdell*, written for the four-justice minority by Justice Sutherland. In it, through an exhaustive analysis of the Contract Clause's history, Sutherland convincingly demonstrated that the provision did not allow states "to mitigate hard consequences resulting to debtors from financial or economic exigencies by the impairment of the obligation of contracts of indebtedness." Indeed, Sutherland proved exactly the opposite: that the Contract Clause "was framed and adopted with the specific and studied purpose of preventing legislation designed to relieve debtors *especially* in time of financial distress."†

But, as usual, the dissent undercut itself. Sutherland approvingly recognized "that 'the reservation of essential attributes of sovereign power is also read into contracts'; and that the Legislature cannot 'bargain away the public health or the public morals'. General statutes to put an end to lotteries, the sale or manufacture of intoxicating liquors, the maintenance of nuisances, to protect the public safety, etc., although they have the indirect effect of absolutely destroying private contracts . . . have been uniformly upheld as not violating the

---

* *Webster's New World Dictionary of the American Language* (The World Publishing Company, 1970).

† *Home Building & Loan Ass'n v. Blaisdell*, 290 U.S. 398, 453, 54 S.Ct. 231, 245-246 (1934); emphasis in original.

contract impairment clause.'[6]

Even at its best Sutherland's dissent was, in the end, only a dissent. Hughes's majority opinion carried the day, making *Blaisdell* the second major case in which the Supreme Court had helped government pull the teeth out of the Contract Clause in the name of need over rights.

About a year later, in the *Gold Clause Cases*, Chief Justice Hughes would deal contracts a body blow in the name of the same doctrines.

To put the *Gold Clause Cases* in proper perspective, it is necessary to go back a few steps.

When a lender (e.g., a bank, a bond buyer) parts with money, there are various concerns: that the loan be repaid, that there be security in case of nonpayment, that interest be paid to compensate for use of the money. A major concern—perhaps *the* major concern, especially in inflationary times—is to protect the value of the principal during the period of the loan, so that at repayment the principal is worth the same in terms of buying power as when the loan was made. For example: no matter what the rate of interest, the "buyer" of a $10,000 twenty-year municipal bond (who is, in reality, a lender) will surely see two decades of inflation considerably depreciate the value (i.e., the purchasing power) of the $10,000. Although twenty years later the bond buyer receives back the same *number* of dollars (10,000), the substantially reduced value of those dollars means that they will purchase far less. To compensate, it is possible to include a provision in any loan contract (including a bond) which will increase the *amount* of repayment (the *number* of dollars) in direct proportion to the principal's decrease in *value* (in purchasing power). Since that value was traditionally measured in gold, the contractual provision has been called "the gold clause."

The gold clause was much relied on between the Civil War (when only debt protected by a gold clause had been safe from the scourge of the "greenbacks") and the New Deal. Indeed, on the eve of Franklin Delano Roosevelt's presidency, about $200,000,000 of outstanding loans were covered by gold clauses, which safeguarded the value of that considerable sum from ever-depreciating paper money. At that time, nothing was more important for protecting lender money from depreciation than the gold clause.

But for that reason alone, its days were numbered—and with it, the many contracts in which it was found.

After his election, Roosevelt and his captive Congress moved fast. A Congressional Joint Resolution of June 5, 1933 condemned the gold clause as being "against public policy" and simply expunged it from all existing contracts. With a single stroke of the pen, *the essential term of countless debt instruments had been struck out, and billions in value simply reallocated from one group (lenders) to another (borrowers).

This, of course, raised a serious question: Did the government act constitutionally? In less than two years, the Supreme Court had answered "yes." In his opinion for the Court's majority, Chief Justice Hughes minced no words:

> Contracts, however express, cannot fetter the constitutional authority of the Congress. Contracts may create rights of property, but when contracts deal with a subject matter which lies within the control of the Congress, they have a *congenital infirmity*. Parties cannot remove their transactions from the reach of dominant constitutional power by making contracts about them.*

Just as with legal tender and depression-era mortgages, once a gold clause provision got in the way of government's desire to adjust the contractual status of private parties to help the "needy," it was no longer safe—even with specific constitutional protection.

Neither *Knox* v. *Lee (Legal Tender II), Blaisdell*, nor the *Gold Clause Cases* were the last cases to approve government abrogation of valid private contracts. Later, the Contract Clause turned out to be impotent in an important case involving the sale of real estate.

> [This case] present[s] for our consideration questions relating to the validity of court enforcement of private agreements, generally described as restrictive covenants, which have as their purpose the exclusion of persons of designated race or color from the ownership or occupancy of real property.[7]

So said Chief Justice Fred M. Vinson, in beginning his opinion for

---

* *Gold Clause Cases*, 294 U.S. 240, 307-308, 55 S.Ct. 407, 416 (1935); emphasis added.

the Court in one of the most important, but comparatively little known, Supreme Court decisions of this century, *Shelly* v. *Kraemer.*

In 1911, thirty landowners in a St. Louis, Missouri neighborhood voluntarily entered into a contract with each other concerning property that each of them owned. They all agreed that for fifty years their property could be owned and occupied only by Caucasians. Their written contract was officially recorded, just like a deed, in order that the restrictive covenant which they had created would "run with the land" (i.e., provide notice to, and be effective against, future purchasers of any of the properties, who would be bound by the contract that their predecessors had made). Putting aside the disgusting reason for the contract—out-and-out racism—the restrictive covenant was, in the narrow context of real estate transactions, not unlike a right-of-way given by a property owner to a neighbor. In the normal course of events, the agreement is recorded so as to give notice to the world as well as future purchasers.

Thirty-five years later, Negroes were sold one of the pieces of property, in apparent violation of the 1911 restrictive covenant.

Even though a refusal to sell property solely for racial reasons is ugly, those thirty property owners back in 1911 *had* voluntarily—and contractually—agreed not to. When that contract was breached, some of the property owners went to court to enforce the restrictive covenant.

Eventually, the case reached the Supreme Court of the United States. There, the covenantors contended that, while the *government* could not discriminate for racial reasons, theirs was a purely *private* contract which in no way involved the government. Conceding this, the Court was obliged to hold "that the restrictive agreements standing alone cannot be regarded as a violation of any rights guaranteed [by the Constitution]."[8]

But rather than the case ending there—as it should have—it was only beginning.

Where was the Court headed? The tip-off was its pointed qualification that the restrictive covenant was constitutional "standing alone." In other words, since the Constitution's Fourteenth Amendment prohibited only *government* from racially discriminating—"No *State* shall . . . deprive any person of life, liberty, or property, without due process of law; nor deny to any person . . . the equal protection of the laws . . . "—and since the *government* had no part in creating the racially restrictive covenant, no Constitutional rights of the Negro purchasers had been violated *up to that point*. But it was not difficult to anticipate what was coming next: " . . . we are called upon to consider whether *enforcement* by state courts of the restrictive agreements . . . may be deemed to be the acts of [the] States . . . "* Even though the state had no hand in *making* the racially restrictive covenant, and thus "standing alone" it was unquestionably valid and violated no one's constitutional rights, the Court saw *this* as the real question: would judicial *enforcement* of the covenant constitute sufficient "state action" to make the private racial discrimination that of the state itself? Here is the Court's answer:

> We have no doubt that there has been state action in these cases in the full and complete sense of the phrase. The undisputed facts disclose that [the Negroes] were willing purchasers of properties upon which they desired to establish homes. The owners of the properties were willing sellers;[†] and contracts of sale were accordingly consmmated. It is clear that but for the active intervention of the state courts, supported by the full panoply of state power [the Negroes] would have been free to occupy the properties . . . without restraint.[9]

Quite true. But what of the right of the covenantors to have their concededly valid private contract enforced in a court of law? What of the fact that the "desires" or "needs" of prospective buyers in a free market are not absolute, but merely something which they can *try* to satisfy? Or the fact that prospective buyers have only such rights in what they seek to purchase as they can acquire through the voluntary consent of the owners—be it land, pencils, bread, or anything else? Indeed, what is the *purpose* of law courts in a society which purports to be based on free choice, if not to implement that choice?

Despite the fact that a racially restrictive covenant embodies the free choice of bigoted landowners, *Shelly* threw these landowners out of court. Narrowly, it held that while a racially restrictive covenant is

---

* *Shelly* v. *Kraemer*, 334 U.S. 1, 18, 68 S.Ct. 836, 844-845 (1948); emphasis added.

†The Court conveniently ignored the unwillingness of the property's original owner, who had entered into the covenant with the understanding that it would continue as a fifty-year condition for the property's purchase.

perfectly valid by itself, society's values, including the Court's, should not permit it to be enforced.

More broadly, *Shelly* held that there is no contractually *enforceable* right of private discrimination based on race—and probably not on religion, alienage, or gender.

Indeed, looking back at *Knox* v. *Lee (Legal Tender II)*, *Blaisdell*, the *Gold Clause Cases*, and *Shelly*, it is hardly possible to miss the message that the Supreme Court has sent out so loud and clear on the subject of contracts generally: rights can quickly be sacrificed to need. Despite Constitutional guarantees, the right of private contract is more apparent than real, since it exists subject to the arbitrary dictates of the altruist-collectivist ethics, and since it can be wiped out by the stroke of a statist pen.

In short, there is no *right* of private contract.

4.

RELIGION

---

*Congress shall make no law... prohibiting the free
exercise [of religion]....*
> —*Amendment 1, Constitution of
> the United States of America*

Because religion and religious values permeate our culture, not only in regular worship but in education, art, law, literature and virtually every other aspect of our lives, freedom of religion is one constitutionally guaranteed right that most Americans are acutely aware of.

Less well known is the reason why religious freedom is protected by the First Amendment.

> The oppressive measures adopted, and the cruelties and punishments inflicted, by the governments of Europe for many ages, to compel parties to conform, in the religious beliefs and modes of worship, to the views of the most numerous sect, and the folly of attempting in that way to control the mental operations of persons, and enforce an outward conformity to a prescribed standard, led to the adoption of [the free exercise of religion guarantee].[1]

Given this reason for guaranteeing religious freedom in America, and given that guarantee's unconditional statement in the Constitution—"Congress shall make no law . . . ."—one might assume that the right was secure.

Not so.

Two very different cases—one involving a nineteenth-century Mormon polygamist, the other some twentieth-century Jewish shopkeepers—reveal how, and why, free exercise of religion in America is not quite so free as people may think.

The Mormon Church—officially named the Church of Jesus Christ of Latter-Day Saints—was founded in the United States in 1830, and many of its adherents settled in Utah. Since Utah was a territory prior to its 1896 admission to the Union, federal laws governed there. One of those laws, enacted in 1862, provided that:

> Every person having a husband or wife living, who marries another, whether married or single, in a Territory, or other place over which the [federal government has] jurisdiction, is guilty of bigamy, and shall be punished by a fine of not more than $500, and by imprisonment for a term of not more than five years.[2]

Set squarely against this federal antibigamy statute was the religious *duty* of male Mormons to practice polygamy.

Indeed, the Supreme Court of the United States had acknowledged:

> . . . that this duty was enjoined by different books which [Mormons] believed to be of divine origin . . . that the members of the Church believed that the practice of polygamy was directly enjoined upon the male members thereof by the Almighty God . . . that the failing or refusing to practice polygamy by such male members . . . would be punished, and that the penalty . . . would be damnation in the life to come.[3]

With the federal antibigamy law pushing at him from one side, and his religious duty to practice polygamy pushing from the other, Utah Mormon George Reynolds was in a vise. If he rendered unto Caesar, he affronted God and was damned. If he rendered unto God, Caesar would surely imprison him.

God won the first round. Reynolds, within the ritual of his church, took a second bride.

Caesar, however, was not amused. The federal government indicted Reynolds for violation of its antibigamy statute. He defended the charge by asserting that the First Amendment guaranteed him the right freely to exercise his religion.

Convicted in the territorial courts, Reynolds's case reached the Supreme Court of the United States in 1878.

There, though Chief Justice Waite's enunciation of the issue for the Court was a bit fuzzy (" . . . whether religious belief can be accepted as a justification of an overt act made criminal by the law of the land")[4] the issue itself was clear. The Chief Justice was really asking whether, in light of the free exercise guarantee, a statute could outlaw the required Mormon religious practice of polygamy.

The Court's answer was another victory for Caesar. It unanimously held the federal antibigamy law constitutional, and the religious duty required of Reynolds by his God had to take a back seat to secular considerations. Why?

To support its decision, the Court in *Reynolds* v. *United States* invoked English history—but inadequately. England (a country with its own national church) had never enjoyed a free exercise of religion guarantee, nor even a written constitution, for that matter. The Court invoked the supposed intention of the guarantee's original sponsors— but that was equivocal at best. The Court even resorted to "nosecounting"—with a clear racist implication—to buttress its conclusion that: "Polygamy has always been odious among the Northern and Western Nations of Europe, and, until the establishment of the Mormon Church, was almost exclusively a feature of the life of Asiatic and of African people."[5]

All camouflage. English history and snide racist references aside, the *real* reason the Court reached its conclusion is contained in portions of just two sentences in the Court's twenty-four-page opinion. In one, the Court observed that Congress was "free to reach actions which were in violation of social duties. . . . "[6] In the other, the Court noted that " . . . there never has been a time in any State of the Union when polygamy has not been an offense against society. . . . "[7]

The common denominator here is apparent. What did the Court mean by the traditions of "society"—specifically the morally puritanical majority of Americans whose antipolygamy attitudes spurred Congress to enact the law, the president to approve it, and various courts (up to and including the Supreme Court) to uphold it? By "society," the Court meant the "collective." "Society" (lots of other people, but not the Mormons) opposed polygamy, therefore, society's values had to prevail. Since the Mormon's values, then, were to be sacrificed, the Court was doing so in the name of altruism. Though polygamy involved consenting adults exercising a religious duty whose exercise was guaranteed by the First Amendment, the altruist-collectivist ethics prevailed.

Since few people have ever wanted to practice polygamy, what difference did it make what happened to George Reynolds in 1878? It made a big difference nearly a century later to a man named Abraham Braunfeld and other Orthodox Jewish retail store owners in Philadelphia.

In the late 1950s Braunfeld and others ran afoul of state-enacted "Blue Laws," which, among other proscriptions, prohibited the retail sale of certain items on Sunday. The constitutionality of such mandatory closing laws had never been decided by the Supreme Court, and after several "Blue Laws" cases had worked their way up through various state courts, the High Court reviewed Braunfeld's and three others'. Although the Blue Laws cases make important points about government control of business, government paternalism, and government fostering of religious values, their importance for our present purpose concerns their effect on the free exercise of religion.

The Blue Laws affected religion in a different way than the federal antipolygamy law had in *Reynolds* (where the statute had flatly made unlawful the performance of a religious duty). To understand that difference, one should first understand something about the Blue Laws themselves. Typically, they prohibit all labor, business, and other commercial activity on Sunday. They are also riddled with myriad exceptions: "necessaries" such as bread, milk, gasoline, newspapers, can be sold; sports activities and concerts can be performed; some of the laws apply all day, others only in the morning or afternoon; within a state, different locales may have different prohibitions.

On their face, these kinds of laws arguably would seem to violate at least three major constitutional guarantees: equal protection of the

laws—because the classifications and exemptions are unconstitutionally arbitrary; due process—because often the statutory attempts to
characterize various exemptions are unconstitutionally vague; and the
First/Fourteenth Amendments' "establishment" clause prohibiting
government aid to religion—because Sabbath laws are unconstitutionally rooted in sectarian considerations. All three of these arguments
were actually made to the Supreme Court. All three were rejected.[8]

The Court found no violation of equal protection of the laws
because, it said, legislatures could reasonably find that:

> ... the Sunday sale of the exempted commodities was necessary
> either for the health of the populace or for the enhancement of the
> recreational atmosphere of the day—that a family which takes a
> Sunday ride into the country will need gasoline for the automobile and
> may find pleasant a soft drink or fresh fruit; that those who go to the
> beach may wish ice cream or some other item normally sold there; that
> some people will prefer alcoholic beverages or games of chance to add
> to their relaxation; that newspapers and drug products should always be
> available to the public.[9]

As to the alleged due process vagueness problem, the Court simply
asserted that the exemptions were not vague.

As to the Blue Laws constituting an unconstitutional establishment
of religion—Sunday being the Sabbath of America's predominant
Christian sects—the Supreme Court reached exactly the opposite
conclusion. Though conceding that the laws' genesis *had* been steeped
in religious motives, the Court concluded that sectarian concerns were
no longer the reason for Sunday closing laws. Today, the Court held,
"[t]he legislative plan is plain. It is to compel [!] a day of rest from
work, permitting only activities which are necessary or recreation-
al."[10]

Quite apart from the ominous implications of government having
the power to compel a uniform day of rest (with socially useful
exemptions, of course), and apart from the admittedly sectarian origin
of that idea, the Blue Laws still presented a subtle but major issue of
freedom of religion. That issue was decided in the *Gallagher* and
Braunfeld cases.

Typically, the Sunday closing laws in both Massachusetts and
Pennsylvania prohibited a wide range of activities, many exceptions

were provided, and violation of the law, especially on a continuing basis, was harshly punished.

In *Gallagher*, four stockholders-officers-directors of the Springfield, Massachusetts Crown Kosher Super Market were Orthodox Jews, as were many of their customers. Since the Orthodox Jewish religion requires its adherents to refrain from commercial activity on the Sabbath—from sundown on Friday to sundown on Saturday—Crown regularly closed during that period. To compensate for the loss of business, the supermarket remained open on Sunday, when it did about one-third of its total weekly business. Doing business on Sunday is what caused Crown's run-in with the Blue Laws.

In *Braunfeld*, though the facts paralleled *Gallagher*, Orthodox Jewish retail clothing and home furnishings merchants were in an even worse position. For them, being forced by the Blue Laws to close on Sunday would not merely be inconvenient, it would be financially devastating. The merchants alleged, and the Court accepted as true, that Sunday closing would impair their ability to earn a livelihood. Braunfeld would be forced out of business.

The year was 1961, Earl Warren was Chief Justice, Douglas, and Black were the senior justices, and Brennan filled out the liberal quartet at the Court's core. Needing only five votes to prevail, and with Frankfurter still on the Bench and Stewart often found in the liberals' corner, the Sabbath observers had some reason to be optimistic, no matter how Clark, Harlan, and Whittaker might vote.

As things turned out, that optimism would have been misplaced. In all four cases, no violation of equal protection, due process, separation of church and state, or freedom of religion was found. The author of the majority opinions was the vaunted liberal Chief Justice, Earl Warren.

In *Gallagher*, Warren framed the issue this way:

> Crown alleges that if it is required by law to abstain from business on Sunday, then, because its owners' religion demands closing from sundown Friday to sundown Saturday, Crown will be open only four and one-half days a week, thereby suffering extreme economic disadvantage. Crown's Orthodox Jewish customers allege that because their religious beliefs forbid their shopping on the Jewish Sabbath, the statutes effect is to deprive them, from Friday afternoon until Monday of each week, of the opportunity to purchase the kosher food sanctioned

by their faith. The Orthodox rabbis allege that the statutes' effect greatly complicates their task of supervising the condition of kosher meat.[11]

The free exercise of religion issue in *Braunfeld* was substantially the same. Addressing it, Warren began with a well-established principle. "As pointed out in *Reynolds*," he said, "legislative power over mere opinion is forbidden but it may reach people's actions when they are found to be in violation of *important social duties* or subversive of good order, even when the actions are demanded by one's religion."* Next, Warren reinforced the *Reynolds* precedent with other authorities, including Thomas Jefferson, to support the proposition that although religious *belief* was unreachable by government, religious *practice* could be regulated, even prohibited. In the latter event, as George Reynolds had learned nearly a century before, one had "the choice . . . of either abandoning his religious principle or facing criminal prosecution."[12] Since that kind of a choice had already been held constitutional nearly a hundred years earlier, what would the Court do about the Blue Laws, which in no way directly legislated concerning the Jewish Sabbath?

That was exactly the point Warren made next. The Blue Laws, he said, do

> not make unlawful any religious practice of [Braunfeld or the other Orthodox Jews]; the Sunday law simply regulates a secular activity and, as applied to [them], operates so as to make the practice of their religious beliefs more expensive. Furthermore, the law's effect does not inconvenience all members of the Orthodox Jewish faith but only those who believe it necessary to work on Sunday. And even these are not faced with as serious a choice as forsaking their religious practices or subjecting themselves to criminal prosecution. Fully recognizing that the alternatives open to [Braunfeld and the others]—retaining their present occupations and incurring economic disadvantage or engaging in some other commercial activity which does not call for either Saturday or Sunday labor—may well result in some financial sacrifice in order to observe their religious beliefs, still the option is wholly different than when the legislation attempts to make a religious practice itself unlawful.[13]

---

* *Braunfeld* v. *Brown*, 366 U.S. 599, 603-604, 81 S.Ct. 1144, 1146 (1961); emphasis added.

Reynolds, of course, had been obliged to "sacrifice" his religious principles on the altar of society's conviction that monogamy was the collective norm, and that polygamy was immoral. To what, then, were Braunfeld's and his coreligionists' religious principles to be sacrificed? Chief Justice Warren made no secret of the Court's answer:

> . . . we cannot find a State without power to provide a weekly respite from all labor and, at the same time, to set one day of the week apart from the others as a day of rest, repose, recreation and tranquility—a day when the hectic tempo of everyday existence ceases and a more pleasant atmosphere is created, a day which all members of the family and community have the opportunity to spend and enjoy together, a day on which people may visit friends and relatives who are not available during working days, a day when the weekly laborer may best regenerate himself. This is particularly true in this day and age of increasing state concern with public welfare legislation.[14]

To accommodate everyone else's need for a uniform day of "rest," then, Sabbath observers could either violate their faith, or go out of business—it was as simple as that.

Warren was joined in his opinion for the Court's majority by Justices Black, Clark, Frankfurter, Harlan, and Whittaker. There were two dissenting opinions: Justice Brennan wrote one (in which Justice Stewart joined); Justice Douglas the other. Although both dissents did conclude that the Blue Laws unconstitutionally violated an Orthodox Jew's right freely to exercise his or her religion, neither opinion should have been taken as vindication by Sabbath observers—or by anyone who understood the meaning of rights.

Brennan agreed with the majority about what issue *Gallagher* and *Braunfeld* presented, but he expressed it more nakedly: "whether a State may put an individual to a choice between his business and his religion."[15] One would naturally assume, Brennan being in the dissent, that his answer was "no." Actually, it was "sometimes." Even though Brennan had dissented, he did not believe that freedom of religious practice was inviolate. On the contrary, Brennan asked: "[w]hat overbalancing [societal] need is so weighty in the constitutional scale that it justifies this substantial, though indirect, limitation of [the Orthodox Jews'] freedom?"[16] The implication of these questions, of course, could not have been clearer: a "weighty" social consideration in favor of the Blue Laws *would* tip Brennan's scale onto the side of constitutionality. What, for example? Brennan answered the question himself: " . . . the desire to stamp out a practice deeply abhorred by society [sound familiar?], such as polygamy as in Reynolds. . . . "[17] With this explanatory observation, Justice Brennan added a spiritual tenth vote to the Court's already unanimous 1878 *Reynolds* decision, conceding that even though the Blue Laws severely impinged on the Sabbath observers' religious practices, the statutes would be constitutional if the importance of a uniform Sunday closing was deeply enough felt by society. By the collective. In *Gallagher* and *Braunfeld*, said Brennan "[i]t is not even the [state] interest in seeing that everyone rests one day a week [apparently a sufficiently important state interest], for [the Sabbath observers'] religion requires that they take such a rest. It is the mere convenience of having everyone rest on the same day."[18]

In the end, Brennan's dissent came down to a disagreement with Warren and the Court's majority, not about *whether* society's collective will could force a choice between Caesar and God, but only *when*. "Weighty" societal concerns, like abhorrence of polygamy, *were* acceptable constitutional justifications; "mere convenience" was not. Steering one's rights between the storm of "weightiness" and the calm of "mere convenience" is never an easy task. If free exercise of religion must depend on such precise navigation, it must necessarily always be at risk.

Interestingly, despite such a clear threat to religious practice, Douglas's dissent endorsed the identical approach that the majority, and Brennan, had—though less obviously. Douglas recognized that:

> . . . the present Sunday laws place Orthodox Jews and Sabbatarians under extra burdens because of their religious opinions or beliefs. Requiring them to abstain from their trade or business on Sunday reduces their work-week to five days, unless they violate their religious scruples. This places them at a competitive disadvantage and penalizes them for adhering to their religious beliefs.[19]

As a result, Douglas concluded that " . . . the penalty [the Blue Laws] place on minorities whose holy day is Saturday constitute . . . state interference with the 'free exercise' of religion."[20]

There were, however, two related and significant wrinkles. One was that Douglas offered nothing at all to support his view that the Blue Laws unconstitutionally interfered with free exercise of religion. The other was that Douglas made no attempt to overcome the *Reynolds* precedent; ironically, he actually embraced it:

> Cases are put where acts that are immoral by our standards but not by the standards of other religious groups are made criminal. That category of cases, until today, has been a very restricted one confined to polygamy . . . and other extreme situations.[21]

Douglas, too, thus accepted the majority's basic premise: that religious practices deemed "immoral" by prevailing social standards—though the instances be "very restricted," and limited to "extreme situations"— *could* be made unlawful. Regrettably, Douglas's only quarrel with the *Gallagher* and *Braunfeld* majority was one of application, not principle. The state's concerns, unlike in *Reynolds*, were just not weighty enough for Douglas's tastes. If they had been, both Brennan and Douglas probably would have voted with the majority, making the decisions unanimous.

When the meaning of *Gallagher* and *Braunfeld* is considered together with that of *Reynolds*, the Supreme Court's message is once again unmistakable: society's collective values, if deemed important enough by the Court, can be implemented at the cost of sacrificing the individual's right freely to exercise his or her religion. This sort of decision making rewrites the Bill of Rights. Instead of providing that "Congress shall make no law . . . prohibiting the free exercise of religion," the First Amendment now seems to be saying: "God shall make no law interfering with the state's requirement that one render unto Caesar."

5.

SPEECH

_Be a craftsman in speech that thou mayest be strong,
for the strength of one is in the tongue, and speech is
mightier than all fighting._

—_Maxims of Ptah Hotep_

Of all the constitutional guarantees found in our Bill of Rights, the
First Amendment's protection of freedom of speech is probably the
best known. Unfortunately, it is also the least understood. Contrary to
popular belief, the First Amendment was never intended to allow, nor
has it ever allowed, truly free speech in America.

For example, although the Massachusetts constitution of 1780—
adopted only a few years after our Declaration of Independence—
contained a free speech guarantee, at least three political libel
convictions were obtained in that commonwealth between 1799 and
1803. Both the Pennsylvania constitution of 1790 and the Delaware
constitution of 1792—enacted at virtually the same time as the federal
Bill of Rights—expressly imposed liability for "abuse" of the right of
free speech. Even Virginia—home of Washington, Jefferson, Madi-

son, Patrick Henry, John Marshall—had enacted a law in 1792 dealing with the "abusive" exercise of speech.

Some of the Founding Fathers were not advocates of fully free speech. For example, Thomas Jefferson—author of the Declaration of Independence and third president of the United States—was not a free speech absolutist. When, in a letter to Abigail Adams, Jefferson condemned the notorious Sedition Act of 1798—which had crudely punished certain political speech and sent not a few anti-Federalist editors to jail—his opposition was based on a "state's rights" position, not on any belief in an unconditional right of free speech. On the contrary, Jefferson contended only that "[t]he First Amendment . . . reflected a limitation upon *Federal* power, leaving the right [sic] to enforce restrictions on speech to the States."*

Jefferson went even further in 1803, writing to the governor of Pennsylvania that "the federalists having failed in destroying freedom of the press by their gag-law, seem to have attacked it in an opposite direction; that is by pushing its licentiousness and its lying to such a degree of prostitution as to deprive it of all credit. * * * This is a dangerous state of things, and the press ought to be restored to its credibility if possible. The restraints provided by the laws of the States are sufficient for this, if applied. And I have, therefore, long thought that a few prosecutions of the most prominent offenders would have a wholesome effect in restoring the integrity of the presses. Not a general prosecution, for that would look like a persecution; but a selected one."†

Thomas Jefferson was not alone in his belief that speech could be censored and that, *occasionally*, disagreeable speakers should be prosecuted. The idea persisted. For over a century, the right of free speech was generally regarded as not absolute. Indeed, not until early in the twentieth century did the Supreme Court of the United States first have occasion to address the subject specifically.

During World War I, an antiwar activist named Schenck (and others) produced and distributed an antidraft handbill. One side of it

---

* *Dennis v. United States*, 341 U.S. 494, 522, 71 S.Ct. 857, 873 (1951); emphasis added.

† *The Constitution of the United States of America* (U.S. Government Printing Office, 1964), p. 864.

claimed that the Conscription Act constituted slavery and involuntary servitude in violation of the Thirteenth Amendment to the Constitution of the United States. "In impassioned language it intimated that conscription was despotism in its worst form and a monstrous wrong against humanity in the interest of Wall Street's chosen few. It said, 'Do not submit to intimidation,' but in form at least confined itself to peaceful measures such as a petition for repeal of the act. The other ... side of the sheet was headed 'Assert Your Rights.' It [claimed that the Constitution was violated by anyone who] refused to recognize 'your right to assert your opposition to the draft,' and went on, 'If you do not assert and support your rights, you are helping to deny or disparage rights which it is the solemn duty of all citizens and residents of the United States to retain.'[*] It described the arguments on the other side as coming from cunning politicians and a mercenary capitalist press, and even silent consent to the conscription law as helping to support an infamous conspiracy. It denied the power to send our citizens away to foreign shores to shoot up the people of other lands, and added that words could not express the condemnation such cold-blooded ruthlessness deserves ... winding up 'You must do your share to maintain, support and uphold the rights of the people of this country.' "[1]

As a result of the handbill's distribution, the defendants were charged with conspiring to violate the Espionage Act of June 15, 1917,[2] by attempting to cause, and by causing, insubordination in the military and naval forces, and by obstructing the government's recruiting and enlistment efforts. In their defense, Schenck and the others invoked the freedom of speech supposedly guaranteed by the First Amendment's injunction that "Congress shall make no law ... abridging the freedom of speech ... " Notwithstanding this seemingly clear constitutional prohibition, the defendants were convicted in a Pennsylvania federal court, and their convictions were affirmed by a unanimous opinion of the Supreme Court written by Justice O.W. Holmes, Jr. After all, said Holmes, "[w]hen a nation is at war many things that might be said in time of peace are such a hindrance to its

---

* If the "deny or disparage rights" and "retained by the people" formulations sound familiar, it is because they are a paraphrase of the Constitution's Ninth Amendment: "The enumeration in the Constitution of certain rights shall not be construed to deny or disparage others retained by the people."

effort that their utterance will not be endured so long as men
fight . . . "[3]

Schenck was an important decision not only because it held that, in
a crunch, even speech could be suppressed for the "common good,"
but because it became the foundation for the Court's infamous "Smith
Act" decision three decades later.

In that case, American communists were charged not with actually
having committed substantive violent acts, but with having conspired:

> (1) to organize as the Communist Party of the United States of
> America a society . . . of persons who . . . advocate the overthrow and
> destruction of . . . the United States by force and violence, and (2)
> knowingly and wilfully to advocate . . . the duty and necessity of
> overthrowing and destroying . . . the United States by force and
> violence.[4]

In upholding their convictions against a First Amendment free
speech defense, the Chief Justice of the Supreme Court stated
categorically that:

> Speech is not an absolute, above and beyond control by the legislature
> when its judgment, subject to review here, is that certain kinds of speech
> are so *undesirable* as to warrant criminal sanction. *Nothing is more
> certain in modern society than the principle that there are no absolutes*
> [I wonder if the Chief Justice was absolutely certain of that?] . . . To
> those who would paralyze our Government in the face of impending
> threat by encasing it in a semantic straitjacket we must reply that *all
> concepts are relative.**

If from the very first days of this nation restraints on speech were
not uncommon, if no less a patriot than Founding Father Thomas
Jefferson believed that states could censor speech and that a selective
prosecution now and then of an unpopular speaker was desirable, if
during World War I antidraft activists could be sent to jail for quoting
the Ninth and Thirteenth Amendments, if American communists
could be imprisoned not for throwing bombs but for merely agreeing to
organize and advocate, if there are no absolutes and all concepts—
such as freedom, liberty and rights—are relative, should anyone be

---

* *Dennis v. United States*, 341 U.S. 494, 508, 74 S.Ct. 857, 867 (1950); emphasis added.

surprised that truly free speech has never existed in our country?

Indeed, even while lauding the great values of the First Amendment, and perhaps elevating them above other Constitutional guarantees, the Court has simultaneously undercut those values by acknowledging the existence of a higher interest:

> The case confronts us again with the duty our system places on this Court to say where the individual's freedom ends and the State's power begins. Choice on that border, now as always delicate, is perhaps more so where the usual presumption supporting legislation is balanced by the preferred place given in our scheme to the great, the indispensable democratic freedoms secured by the First Amendment.
>
> * * *
>
> That priority gives these liberties a sanctity and a sanction not permitting dubious intrusions. . . .
>
> For these reasons any attempt to restrict those liberties must be justified by clear *public interest.* . . . *

Schenck, *Dennis* and *Thomas* introduce the speech material which is the subject of this chapter. They illustrate *that* Americans have always been denied the right of truly free speech in the area of political expression. To a lesser extent, the three cases suggest *why*. For a more thorough understanding of the "why," two other categories of speech must be examined. One is so-called "commercial speech." The other is speech concerning sexual matters.

The Supreme Court of the United States has long been expert at creating spurious, seemingly antithetical distinctions, e.g., "personal rights" versus "property rights"; "due process" versus "rudimentary due process"; "affirmative action" versus "racial quotas." Among these distinctions none has been more spurious than "regular" speech versus "commercial" speech.

An interesting and instructive example of commercial speech arose in a New York case about four decades ago. Back in the early 1940s, a New York entrepreneur who owned a submarine wanted to conduct submarine tours from a city pier. After the authorities denied him permission, he had handbills printed. One side carried an advertising

---

* *Thomas v. Collins*, 323 U.S. 516, 529-530, 65 S.Ct. 315, 322-323 (1945); emphasis added.

message promoting the tour, the other a protest against the city's denial of permission to use the pier. The city, attempting to stop the handbilling, invoked a law prohibiting the distribution of any "handbill, circular . . . or other advertising matter whatsoever in or upon any street."

Eventually the Supreme Court was confronted with this question: were the handbills a form of protected speech, since they contained a combination of "commercial" and "noncommercial" (i.e., "ideological") matter? The Court held they were not.[5] While conceding that the First Amendment forbade the city's banning of *all* handbilling on public thoroughfares—and even the protest part of the submarine handbills *standing alone*—the Court concluded that the First Amendment imposed "no such restraint on government as respects purely commercial advertising."[6] *Valentine*, which apparently saw the handbills' combined content as being sufficiently commercial to warrant banning, thus created at least two distinct categories of speech. One could be suppressed by government; the other could not.

The distinction in *Valentine* was underscored by two cases which followed it. In *Martin* v. *Struthers*[7] the Court held that freedom of speech had been infringed by a municipal ordinance forbidding door-to-door distribution of leaflets publicizing a *religious* meeting, because "no element of the commercial" was involved.[8] Yet in *Breard* v. *Alexandria*[9] the Court found no freedom of speech violation by an ordinance prohibiting door-to-door solicitation of *magazine subscriptions*. "The selling," the Court reasoned, "brings into the transaction a *commercial* feature."*

The relegation of so-called commercial speech to second-class constitutional status—despite the First Amendment's clear proscription that government "shall make no law . . . abridging the freedom of speech"—was an accepted fact of First Amendment life for more than thirty years.[10] During that period, while the *Valentine* case excluded commercial speech from the protection that the First Amendment afforded to most other types of communication, some justices, especially Douglas, were becoming increasingly uncomfortable. Douglas's dilemma was that, on the one horn, he viewed the First Amendment as an absolute bar to government interference with the

---

* *Breard* v. *Alexandria*, 341 U.S. 622, 642, 71 S.Ct. 920, 932 (1951); emphasis added.

highly personal right of speech[11] but that, on the other, his animus toward so-called property rights was extensive.[12] So Douglas's problem, fundamentally, was whether commercial speech was commerce or whether it was speech. Was it merely part of the marketplace, where regulation in the public interest was accepted, if not mandatory? Or was it part of the rarefied atmosphere, where ideas were communicated? Although Douglas had gone along with the majority in *Valentine*, by the time of *Cammarano* v. *United States*[13] seventeen years later, he was expressing doubts. Those doubts about the commercial speech doctrine were merely reflective of much deeper questions at the core of all American constitutional law: how could a supposedly free country be premised on personal sacrifice in the name of majoritarian values—i.e., on the altruist-collectivist ethics? How could individual rights be subordinated to the needs of society?

The answer given by the Supreme Court, when it finally discarded the commercial speech doctrine, was no cause for celebration.

In Virginia, pharmacists were prohibited from advertising the price of prescription drugs, and in the mid-1970s the law was challenged constitutionally. But not by muzzled pharmacists, invoking their right to free speech. Interestingly, the attack on the Virginia law came instead from prescription drug *consumers*. They claimed that since prescription drug prices varied widely, they would benefit greatly if advertising were freely allowed, making it possible for them to shop around for the lowest price.[14] The basic issue for the Supreme Court was whether the Virginia law was constitutional, but the way in which the Court formulated that issue was very significant:

> Our question is whether speech which does "no more than propose a commercial transaction" [citation omitted] is so removed from any "exposition of ideas" [citation omitted] and from " 'truth, science, morality, and arts in general, in its diffusion of liberal sentiments on the administration of government,' " [citation omitted], that it lacks all protection.[15]

The implication of this question went far beyond the limited subject of commercial speech. The Court's formulation of the question to be decided in the *Virginia State Board of Pharmacy* case itself reveals exactly what will separate protected from unprotected speech: its *social utility*. Whether commercial speech generally, or any manifestation of it in particular, is or is not protected, is relatively unimportant compared to the socially based criterion by which protection is judged. *That* the *Virginia State Board of Pharmacy* case protected the advertising of prescription drug prices, and perhaps all truthful and legal commercial speech,[16] is not nearly as significant as *why* it did. As to that, the Court was quite explicit, and its reasons had noticeably little or nothing to do with the *pharmacists'* free speech.

Focusing not on the rights of the pharmacists but on the needs of the consumers, the Court candidly admitted that:

> As to the particular consumer's interest in the free flow of commercial information, that interest may be as keen, if not keener by far, than his interest in the day's most urgent political debate. [The consumers'] case in this respect is a convincing one. Those whom the suppression of prescription drug price information hits the hardest are the *poor*, the *sick*, and particularly the *aged*. A disproportionate amount of their income tends to be spent on prescription drugs; yet they are the least able to learn, by shopping from pharmacist to pharmacist, where their scarce dollars are best spent. When drug prices vary as strikingly as they do, information as to who is charging what becomes more than a convenience. It could mean the alleviation of physical pain or the enjoyment of basic necessities.
>
> Generalizing, society also may have a strong interest in the free flow of commercial information.[17]

In short, the *needs* of the poor, sick, and aged (as well as the interests of "society" generally) were the Court's yardstick in measuring what was, and was not, allowable free speech. The unalienable *right* of the pharmacists freely to communicate was not even an issue. That the former's needs justified the latter's speech was—is—a dangerous notion. To make social utility (i.e., who needs what, and how much) the criterion for free speech is to place it under government control *and* in the service of others. It is too easy for government to decide that no need exists for consumers to hear about a wide variety of topics, and, from there, that no right exists to speak about them. It is too easy to assert that the needs of the poor, the sick, the aged—of society—have changed, thus allowing still other speech to be stifled. Indeed, that is exactly what happened to sexual expression.

Just as the strength of steel is best measured under stress, meaningful tests of principle come not over the best of issues but over the worst. One such test has assumed the proportions of a major battle in the war between individual rights and altruism-collectivism-statism. It has been fought on the grimy field of pornography. But as Ayn Rand once observed, although it

> is not very inspiring to fight for the freedom of the purveyors of pornography or their customers . . . in the transition to statism, every infringement of human rights has begun with the suppression of a given right's least attractive practitioners. In this case, the disgusting nature of the offenders makes it a good test of one's loyalty to a principle.*

The principle to which Rand referred—the right to the free expression of sexual material, even if society deems it pornographic or obscene—has been under relentlessly successful attack in the Supreme Court of the United States for nearly four decades. The story began in the early 1940s with a Jehovah's Witness in New Hampshire. After calling a policeman "a God damned racketeer" and "a damned fascist," the Witness got into a fight on the sidewalk. Charged with the offense of "fighting words,"† Chaplinsky was convicted because the New Hampshire court interpreted the law to prohibit "words likely to cause an average addressee to fight," "face-to-face words 'plainly likely' to cause a breach of the peace by the addressee."

Believing that Chaplinsky's words were "likely to provoke the average person to retaliation,"[18] the Supreme Court of the United States unanimously upheld his conviction.

Putting aside the *Chaplinsky* case's implications for free speech generally, and for the "fighting words" category of political speech in particular, something else of far greater importance emerged from that decision. In the course of his opinion for the Court, Justice Murphy observed in passing that:

> There are certain well-defined and narrowly limited classes of speech, the prevention and punishment of which have never been thought to

---

* *The Ayn Rand Letter*, "Censorship: Local and Express," Vol. II, No. 23, August 23, 1973, p. 2.

† "No person shall address any offensive, derisive or annoying word to any other person who is lawfully in any street or other public place, nor call him by any offensive or derisive name."

raise any Constitutional problem. These include the *lewd* and *obscene*, the profane, the libelous, and the insulting or "fighting" words—those by which their very utterance inflict injury or tend to incite an immediate breach of the peace. It has been well observed that such utterances are no essential part of any exposition of ideas, and are of such slight social value as a step to truth that any benefit that may be derived from them is clearly outweighed by the social interest in order and morality.*

There were two small points wrong with Justice Murphy's notion that the prohibition of certain kinds of speech had never bothered anyone. For one thing, it was untrue—there have always been First Amendment absolutists [among them, the author of this book] who read the Constitution's bar of "no law" abridging speech to mean literally just that. Such people have been bothered a lot.[†] For another, Murphy seemed to imply that if no one did object, then preventing and punishing certain speech would be an acceptable practice. This is tantamount to evaluating rights by counting noses.

Much more important, however, is that, at the core of Murphy's statement lay three pernicious, though well-entrenched, ideas: that morality is defined by societal values; that the only moral utterances are those which are an "exposition of ideas" or "a step to truth"; that "the lewd and obscene" are beyond the pale.

What utter presumptuousness! What a naked invocation of the idea that one's rights come from, and are subordinate to, society. That it is government's proper function to violate individual rights for the common good.

Such gratuitous observations by the Court about morality, society and obscenity were wholly unnecessary to the decision in *Chaplinsky* (which was not even an obscenity case), and thus supposedly of no precedential value in obscenity cases which would come later.

Nevertheless, when, fifteen years later, the Court did accept an obscenity case, *Chaplinsky* played an important role.

The majority opinion in *Roth* v. *United States* and *Alberts* v.

---

* *Chaplinsky* v. *New Hampshire*, 315 U.S. 568, 571-572, 62 S.Ct. 766, 769 (1942); emphasis added.

[†] Though Justices Douglas and Black had big reputations as First Amendment absolutists, they had joined the *Chaplinsky* majority. Perhaps they viewed it simply as a disorderly conduct case, not involving speech.

California[19] was written by the liberal Justice Brennan. In upholding both antiobscenity statutes (one federal and one state) he built his opinion on four cornerstones. First, "expressions found in numerous opinions indicate that this Court has always *assumed* that obscenity is not protected by the freedoms of speech and press."* Second, in light of American colonial history (pre-Constitution) "it is apparent that the unconditional phrasing of the First Amendment was not *intended* to protect every utterance."† Third, "implicit in the history of the First Amendment is the rejection of obscenity as utterly without redeeming social importance. This rejection for that reason is mirrored in the *universal judgment* that obscenity should be restrained, reflected in the international agreement of over 50 nations, in the obscenity laws of all of the [then] 48 states, and in the 20 obscenity laws enacted by the Congress from 1842 to 1956." Fourth, and the nearest the Court could get to precedent, "[t]his is the same judgment expressed by this court in *Chaplinsky* v. *New Hampshire* . . . "‡

So, because of repeated "assumptions" by the Court, an analysis of *pre*-Constitutional history, an "implication" in the First Amendment's history and a "universal judgment" condemning obscenity, *and* the *Chaplinsky dictum*, "obscenity" was held "not within the area of constitutionally protected speech or press."[20]

Defining unprotected "obscene material" as that "which deals with sex in a manner appealing to prurient interest,"** the Court was quick to assert that since "sex and obscenity are not synonymous"[21] certain expression of a sexual nature would be protected—but even then only if two criteria were satisfied:

> All ideas having even the slightest social importance—unorthodox

---

* *Roth* v. *United States, Alberts* v. *California*, 354 U.S. 476, 481, 77 S.Ct. 1304, 1307 (1957); emphasis added.

† *Roth* v. *United States, Alberts* v. *California*, 354 U.S. 476, 483, 77 S.Ct. 1304, 1308 (1957); emphasis added.

‡ *Roth* v. *United States, Alberts* v. *California*, 365 U.S. 476, 484, 77 S.Ct. 1304, 1309 (1957); emphasis added. Since *Chaplinsky* was not an obscenity case, Murphy's passing reference in that case to "the lewd and obscene" was a mere *dictum*, having no precedential value and hardly constituting a "judgment."

** *Roth* v. *United States, Alberts* v. *California*, 354 U.S. 476, 487, 77 S.Ct. 1304, 1310 (1957). The Court footnoted Webster's definition of "prurient": " . . . itching, longing; uneasy with desire or longing . . . "

ideas, controversial ideas, even ideas hateful to the prevailing climate of opinion—have the full protection of the [Constitutional] guarantees, unless excludable because they encroach upon the limited area of more important interests.[22]

Brennan was saying—and the Court was holding—two things: "obscenity" was unprotected speech under any and all circumstances; and other sexual expression was also unprotected *unless* society deemed it of at least some importance. Even then, such semi-important expression could be suppressed if there were "more important" societal interests at stake.

In sum, as Justice Douglas was to observe in a later obscenity case:

In *Roth* v. *United States* . . . [the Court] ruled that "[o]bscene material is material which deals with sex in a manner appealing to prurient interest." . . . Obscenity, it was said, was rejected by the First Amendment because it is "utterly without redeeming social importance." . . . The presence of a "prurient interest" was to be determined by "contemporary community standards."[23]

Roth established that there was a category of unprotected speech called obscenity, which was to be identified by reference to the sexual premises of one's friends and neighbors. The stage was now set for the Supreme Court of the United States to assume the role of High Court of Censorship.

That role has built-in problems—exemplified by a candid observation on the part of Justice Stewart in *Jacobellis* v. *Ohio*.[24] In that case, though there was no clear-cut majority position, the Court did hold that a motion picture was *not* obscene under the *Roth* standard. But it was Justice Stewart who underscored the problems inherent in all obscenity cases. He admitted that the Court was "faced with the task of trying to define what may be indefinable."[25] As for his own test for specific examples of alleged obscenity, the best he could come up with was: "I know it when I see it, and the motion picture involved in this case is not that."[26]

With "I know it when I see it" as more or less the Constitutional test for obscenity, the Court next confronted the "Fanny Hill" case, *Memoirs* v. *Massachusetts*.[27] There, the *Roth* test was reformulated:

. . . three elements must coalesce: it must be established that (a) the dominant theme of the material taken as a whole appeals to a prurient interest in sex; (b) the material is patently offensive because it affronts contemporary community standards relating to the description or representation of sexual matters; and (c) the material is utterly without redeeming social value.[28]

So while *Roth* had merely *presumed* that "obscenity" was "utterly without redeeming social importance," *Memoirs* now required prosecutors to *affirmatively establish* that "obscene" material was utterly without redeeming social value.

Either way, to make the test of free expression depend on whether it affronts or has value to *others*, is explicitly to endorse the altruist-collectivist premise (one's rights are derived from society), and to implement that premise by statism (government forcing individuals to conform to a social norm).

After *Memoirs*, the Supreme Court justices were in disarray.

By 1967 the following views concerning obscenity had emerged: Mr. Justice Black and Mr. Justice Douglas consistently maintained that government is wholly powerless to regulate any sexually oriented matter on the ground of its obscenity. * * * Mr. Justice Harlan, on the other hand, believed that the Federal Government in the exercise of its enumerated powers could control the distribution of "hard core" pornography, while the States were afforded more latitude to "[ban] any material which, taken as a whole has been reasonably found in state judicial proceedings to treat with sex in a fundamentally offensive manner, under rationally established criteria for judging such material."

* * * Mr. Justice Stewart regarded "hard core" pornography as the limit of both federal and state power. * * *

The view that . . . enjoyed the most, but not majority, support was an interpretation of *Roth* . . . adopted by Mr. Chief Justice Warren, Mr. Justice Fortas, and [Mr. Justice Brennan] in *Memoirs*. * * * Even this formulation, however, concealed differences of opinion [e.g., whether the "community standards" were national or local]. * * * Moreover, it did not provide a definition governing all situations. See *Mishkin* v. *New York* * * * (prurient interest defined in terms of a sexual group); *Ginzburg* v. *United States* * * * ("pandering" [as] probative evidence in close cases). See also *Ginsberg* v. *New York* * * * (obscenity for juveniles). Nor, finally, did it ever command a majority of the Court. Aside from the other views described above, Mr. Justice Clark believed that "social importance" could only "be considered together with evidence that the material in question appeals to prurient interest and is patently offensive." * * * Similarly, Mr. Justice White regarded "a publication to be obscene if its predominant theme appeals to the prurient interest in a manner exceeding customary limits of candor * * * and regarded " 'social importance' * * * not [as] relevant only to determining the predominant prurient interest of the material. * * * "[29]

Given this murky confusion about the limits of sexually oriented speech, the Court had trouble coping with the increased volume of "obscenity" cases coming its way as a result of *Roth* and *Memoirs*. So the Supreme Court automated its approach, much like a factory manufacturing widgets might have done. Beginning with a 1967 case, *Redrup* v. *New York*,[30] the Court looked closely at lower court convictions for the dissemination of allegedly obscene materials. If at least five justices, using their own individual tests (whatever they were), believed the materials were not obscene, the conviction would be summarily reversed—without a written opinion, without even identifying which justice had voted on what side. Between 1967 and 1973 no fewer than thirty-one obscenity cases, federal and state, were disposed of in this fashion.

While the Court was tossing out criminal obscenity convictions at a wholesale rate, were those who applauded the results aware of what this meant for individual rights? Consider the overall situation. Federal and state legislatures had enacted, the president and various governors had approved, and eventually the United States Supreme Court had upheld, laws making certain verbal and pictorial utterances on the subject of sex criminal. In case after case, the Supreme Court had taken unto itself an impossible task: deciding whether unknown— and unknowable—contemporary community standards had been employed properly or improperly by juries around the country, to ascertain whether sex had been dealt with in an exciting, offensive manner while utterly lacking any redeeming social value. Based on the assessment by a Court majority of what society wished to be expressed on the subject of sex, some persons were allowed to speak, others were not. Some made fortunes, some lost them. Some were revered as writers, others went to prison. Through it all, the Supreme Court relentlessly implemented "society's" will, as best it could.

Just how much it did, and in the name of what, became painfully apparent in the Court's infamous 1973 obscenity decisions, *Miller* v. *California*[31] and *Paris Adult Theater I* v. *Slayton*.[32]

Miller had been convicted of violating California's criminal obscenity statute by sending certain unsolicited advertising brochures through the mail. Some were received, as it turned out, by people who found them quite offensive. In the words of Chief Justice Burger, who wrote the majority opinions in both *Miller* and *Paris Theater*:

> The brochures advertise four books entitled "Intercourse," "Man-Woman," "Sex Orgies Illustrated," and "An Illustrated History of Pornography," and a film entitled "Marital Intercourse." While the brochures contain some descriptive printed material, primarily they consist of pictures and drawings very explicitly depicting men and women in groups of two or more engaging in a variety of sexual activities, with genitals often prominently displayed.[33]

Ordinarily, as in *Redrup* and the thirty-odd cases which followed it, the Court's task in *Miller* simply would have been to ascertain if at least five justices, for whatever reasons, disagreed with the California community's sexual values. Miller's conviction or acquittal, then, would have depended on whether the sexual values of any five Supreme Court justices agreed or disagreed with the sexual values of Miller's friends and neighbors. If five could be found, the *justices'* sexual values would have barred the sexual values of the friends and neighbors of Mr. Miller from being imposed on him. If not, Miller's conviction would have been upheld.

But *Miller* turned out not to be an ordinary case. " . . . we are called on," said Burger, "to define the standards which must be used to identify obscene material that a State may regulate without infringing on the First Amendment . . . "[34] In other words, a sufficient number of justices had decided to reformulate the *Roth-Memoirs* test, and, it was hoped, to get the Court out of the business of "Redrupizing" the obscenity cases that reached it.

The Chief Justice laid the foundation for abandoning *Redrup* by recognizing that:

> Apart from the initial formulation in the *Roth* case, no majority of the Court has at any given time been able to agree on a standard to determine what constitutes obscene, pornographic material subject to regulation under the States' police power. See, e.g., *Redrup* v. *New*

York . . . We have seen "a variety of views among the members of the Court unmatched in any other course of constitutional adjudication."[35]

He also recognized that "no justification has ever been offered in support of the Redrup 'policy.' . . . " and that "[t]he *Redrup* procedure has cast [the Supreme Court] in the role of an unreviewable board of censorship for the 50 states, subjectively judging each piece of material brought before us."[36]

True. And on that foundation, the Court fashioned a new test:

> . . . (a) whether "the average person, applying contemporary community standards" would find that the work, taken as a whole, appeals to the prurient interest . . . (b) whether the work depicts or describes, in a patently offensive way, sexual conduct specifically defined by the applicable state law; and (c) whether the work, taken as a whole, lacks serious literary, artistic, political, or scientific value.[37]

Though part (a) of the new test—average person, *contemporary community standards*, prurient interest—*seemed* basically unchanged from *Roth-Memoirs*, there was a significant difference. In the past, that collectivist norm, "community standards," was deemed to be *national* in scope. So when local jurors were asked to decide whether materials were prurient, they were supposed to focus on the values of the nation as a whole. *Miller* changed that. The Court, while reiterating the same collectivist principle it had endorsed previously, now directed that it be implemented by a different—and much more limited—audience:

> It is neither realistic nor constitutionally sound to read the First Amendment as requiring that the people of Maine or Mississippi accept public depiction of conduct found tolerable in Las Vegas, or New York City. * * * People in different States vary in their tastes and attitudes, and this diversity is not to be strangled by the absolutism of imposed uniformity.[38]

This was no sensible narrowing of the scope of the "community." Although the Court recognized that people in Los Angeles held different values than people in Long Island, it *failed* to recognize that even *within any given area* people's values differ. Just as it is wrong to impose the supposed standards of a national group on a locality, it is equally wrong to impose that locality's standards on individuals. In both cases, free speech is still suppressed by the values of the group.

Part (b) of the *Miller* test—depiction or description of patently offensive sexual *conduct*—was a slight change from *Memoirs's* "description or representation of sexual matters." Though disclaiming that it was the Court's function to propose regulatory schemes for the states, the Court obligingly managed "to give a few plain examples of what a state statute could define for regulation under part (b) . . . "[39] of the *Miller* test: "Patently offensive representations or descriptions of ultimate sex acts, normal or perverted [?], actual or simulated. . . . Patently offensive representations or descriptions of masturbation, excretory functions, and lewd exhibition of the genitals."[40]

As to the Court's formulation and illustration of this part of the *Miller* test, little need be said. It is hardly the function of a government in the late twentieth century, in a purportedly free country, to concern itself with the depiction or description of sex--whether ultimate, perverted, actual, simulated, or normal.

The rampant collectivism found in the *Miller* test's part (a) (contemporary community standards) shows up with a vengeance in part (c), together with an unmistakable dose of statism. Prurient, patently offensive depiction or description of sexual conduct might yet obtain First Amendment protection *if* such material possessed " 'serious' literary, artistic, political, or scientific value." The Court suggested a safe example: " . . . medical books for the education of physicians and related personally necessarily use graphic illustrations and descriptions of human anatomy."[41]

Of the three parts of the *Miller* obscenity test, the last is by far the worst *per se* and, because of its implications, the most dangerous. It is bad enough that the first two parts institutionalize the collectivist notion that *society* is the judge of prurience and patent offensiveness— and thus the official censor of sexual matter; bad enough that the second part allowed government to dictate what sexual conduct may and may not be depicted and described. But it is sheer folly to set *government* as the arbiter of whether books, magazines, newspapers, radio, television and theater have any value at all, let alone "literary, artistic, political, or scientific" value—or, most ominous of all, "serious" value. This is censorship at its worst. That *Miller* imposed it only in the case of obscenity should comfort no one. The principle has been established. In the future, it may be applied to any kind of expression. The genie, once out of the bottle, can never be coaxed or stuffed back inside.

Censorship is what we had, courtesy of the Supreme Court of the United States. How did the justices attempt to justify it? "The protection given speech and press was fashioned," asserts the majority opinion, "to assure unfettered interchange of ideas for the bringing about of political and social changes desired by the people." Translation: our right of free speech and press has a strictly pragmatic base: to allow the collective to effect change. "[T]he public portrayal," the Court continues, "of hard-core sexual conduct for its own sake, and for the ensuing commercial gain, is a different matter."[42] "We do not see the harsh hand of censorship of ideas—good or bad, sound or unsound—and 'repression' of political liberty lurking in every state regulation of commercial exploitation of human interest in sex."[43] With this statement, the Court arbitrarily removed obscenity from the realm of ideas and tarred it with the brush of "commercialism."

In the companion case to *Miller*, the theme of commercialism was addressed more fully. When the Paris theater exhibited the films "Magic Mirror" and "It All Comes Out in the End," they ran into censorship trouble from local authorities, and ended up in court. The trial judge "assumed 'that obscenity [had been] established,' but stated" that "[i]t appears to the Court that the display of these films in a commercial theater, when surrounded by requisite notice to the public of their nature and by reasonable protection against the exposure of these films to minors, is constitutionally permissible."[44]

The Supreme Court of Georgia disagreed. Though it "assumed that the adult theaters in question barred minors and gave a full warning to the general public of the nature of the films shown," it nevertheless "held that the films were without protection under the First Amendment. . . . [T]he Georgia court stated that 'the sale and delivery of obscene material to willing adults is not protected under the First Amendment.' "[45] This framed the issue pretty well. *Miller* had reiterated that one category of unprotected speech was obscenity, and in order to define it had reformulated the earlier *Roth-Memoirs* test. But one thing *Miller* had not explicitly decided was whether the sexual mores of the community could deprive *consenting adults* of porno-graphic material which they wanted, sought, and obtained.

Chief Justice Burger's answer for the Supreme Court's majority could not have been clearer:

> We categorically disapprove the theory, apparently adopted by the trial judge, that obscene, pornographic films acquire constitutional immunity from state regulation simply because they are exhibited for consenting adults only. This holding [by the Georgia trial judge] was properly rejected by the Georgia Supreme Court. Although we have often pointedly recognized the high importance of the state interest in regulating the exposure of obscene materials to juveniles and unconsenting adults, see *Miller* v. *California* . . . *Redrup* v. *New York* . . . this Court has never declared these to be the only legitimate state interests permitting regulation of obscene material.[46]

Not everyone could be expected to agree, either about what were "legitimate state interests," or why. So in the course of his *Paris* opinion, Burger tried to anticipate, and answer, all possible arguments.

To the obvious objection "that the State of Georgia is . . . attempting to control the minds or thoughts of those who patronize theaters," Burger answered as he had in *Miller*: he excluded obscenity from the realm of protected speech simply by defining protected speech as not including obscenity. "Preventing unlimited display or distribution of obscene material, which by definition lacks any serious literary, artistic, political, or scientific value as communication . . . ," Burger asserted, "is distinct from a control of reason and the intellect."[47]

To the argument that watching obscene movies in a darkened theater was a privacy right not to be interfered with by the state, our conservative Chief Justice answered by invoking precedents provided, ironically, by liberals: "This Court has, on numerous occasions, refused to hold that *commercial* ventures such as a motion-picture house are 'private' for the purpose of civil rights litigation and civil rights statutes. See . . . *Heart of Atlanta Motel, Inc.* v. *United States*. . . . The Civil Rights Act of 1964 specifically defines motion-picture houses and theaters as places of *'public accommodation'* covered by the Act as operations affecting commerce." "Nothing," said Burger, "in this Court's decisions intimates that there is any . . . privacy right . . . to watch obscene movies in places of public accommodation."[48]

The expansive use of the interstate commerce clause, previously used by government to force unwanted customers on unwilling motels and restaurants in the name of "civil rights," was now being used by government to control free expression and consumption of the written and spoken word and screen images, in the name of community morals.

Some chickens from Ollie's Barbecue had finally come home to roost.

To the contention that even if society could implement its sexual values at the expense of others, there had to be at least some showing that obscenity caused *harm*, Burger replied:

> Although there is no conclusive proof of a connection between antisocial behavior and obscene material, the legislature of Georgia could quite reasonably determine that such a connection does or might exist.
>
> From the beginning of civilized societies, legislators and judges have acted on various *unprovable* assumptions.
>
> * * *
>
> If we accept the *unprovable* assumption that a complete education requires the reading of certain books . . . and the well nigh universal belief that good books, plays, and art lift the spirit, improve the mind, enrich the human personality, and develop character, can we then say that a state legislature may not act on the corollary assumption that commerce in obscene books, or public exhibition focused on obscene conduct, have a tendency to exert a corrupting and debasing impact leading to antisocial behavior?*

In summing up these arguments, the Chief Justice asserted: "[t]he fact that a [law] reflects *unprovable* assumptions about what is good for the people, including imponderable aesthetic assumptions, is not a sufficient reason to find that statute unconstitutional."† This was an endorsement of the proposition that censorship—indeed, thought control—could constitutionally rest not only on *unproved* assumptions about whether obscenity caused harm, but on assumptions of causality *which could not be proved*. A startling notion. To support it, Burger pointed out—correctly, and once again ironically—that un-

---

* *Paris Adult Theater I* v. *Slayton*, 413 U.S. 49, 60-61, 63, 93 S.Ct. 2607, 2637, 2638 (1973); emphasis added.

† *Paris Adult Theater I* v. *Slayton*, 413 U.S. 49, 62, 93 S.Ct. 2607, 2638 (1973); emphasis added.

provable assumptions "underlie much lawful state regulation of commercial and business affairs" and "the federal securities and antitrust laws and a host of federal regulations."[49] More liberal precedent, and an interesting point: regulation is regulation. Burger recognized that, in principle, there is no difference between regulating commerce or business and controlling speech or press.

The theater argued that Georgia could not intrude on the film's exhibition because the transaction involved "consenting adults." Burger's answer:

> The state statute books are replete with constitutionally unchallenged laws against prostitution, suicide, voluntary self-mutilation, brutalizing "bare fist" prize fights, and duels, although these crimes may only directly involve "consenting adults." Statutes making bigamy a crime surely cut into an individual's freedom to associate, but few today seriously claim such statutes violate the First Amendment or any other constitutional provision. . . . Consider also . . . adultery . . . fornication . . . "white slavery" . . . billiard halls . . . gambling.[50]

Consider the principle underlying Burger's almost casual observation: subordination of the individual's personal desires, involving one's property, one's body, one's very life, to the values of society. Since this principle allows government to bar prostitution, suicide and all the rest, logically there is no way it can (or should) stop short of barring obscene material which clashes with those same "values of society." In the face of such a clash, Burger makes no secret of why a "decent society" has a "right" to resort to statism:

> The States have the power to make a *morally neutral* judgment that public exhibition of obscene material, or commerce in such material, has a tendency to injure the community as a whole, to endanger the public safety, or to jeopardize, in Mr. Chief Justice Warren's words, the States' "right . . . to maintain a decent society."[51]

This idea is expanded in two other passages of Burger's majority opinion. In one, he explains that among the state's reasons for suppressing obscenity were "the interest of the public in the quality of life and the total community environment, the tone of commerce in the great city centers, and, possibly, the public safety itself."[52] In the other, he draws heavily on a statement by Professor Alexander Bickel (who, ironically, had represented *The New York Times* in its fight against the federal government's attempt to suppress the Pentagon Papers) which addressed what Burger called a "problem of large proportions":

> It concerns the tone of the society, the mode, or to use terms that have perhaps greater currency, the style and quality of life, now and in the future. A man may be entitled to read an obscene book in his room, or expose himself indecently there. . . . We should protect his privacy. But if he demands a right to obtain the books and pictures he wants in the market, and to foregather in public places—discreet, if you will, but accessible to all—with others who share his tastes, *then to grant to him his right is to affect the world about the rest of us, and to impinge on other privacies.* Even supposing that each of us can, if he wishes, effectively avert the eye and stop the ear (which, in truth, we cannot), what is commonly read and seen and heard and done intrudes upon us all, want it or not.*

Pages could be written about these revealing three passages, but for our purposes, the most obvious points must suffice.

First, it is anything but a "morally neutral judgment" to characterize expression as "obscene," to state as an axiom that government has the right to maintain "a decent society," or to conclude that obscenity endangers "the quality of life and the total community environment." According to the Court itself, "obscenity" is the prurient, patently offensive depiction or description of sexual conduct which lacks certain specified serious value. Virtually every element of the *Miller* test—prurience, offensiveness, seriousness—has meaning *only* on the basis of moral judgment, i.e., when measured against values of right and wrong. It is not surprising that the Court would wish to characterize its antiobscenity bias as a "morally neutral judgment," in order not to admit that the position does indeed stem from a very pronounced moral attitude rooted in puritanical, repressed, and religious ideas about sex and sexuality.

Second, in the name of what—if not altruism-collectivism-statism—

---

* *Paris Adult Theater I* v. *Slayton*, 413 U.S. 49, 59, 93 S.Ct. 2607, 2636 (1973); emphasis in original.

does government have the "right" to concern itself with the "decency" of society, the "quality" of life, the total community "environment," and the "tone" of commerce? What do these loose abstractions even mean? *Who* decides what they mean? How to achieve them? Or at what cost? What happens to those of us who disagree?

Third, how is it possible to assert that a consumer of pornography somehow affects others—unless one is *explicitly* endorsing altruism-collectivism-statism?

These questions are rhetorical. It could not be plainer that the Supreme Court's willingness to brand certain forms of expression as "obscene" stems from its consciously held premise that the rights of the individual are subordinate to the needs of society.

Something else in the opinion also needs to be identified because it answers an important question: in the name of exactly *what* is the Court willing to enslave the individual? *Antisodomy laws exist and are upheld, Burger confesses, "to protect the weak, the uninformed, the unsuspecting, and the gullible from the exercise of their own volition."**

When all is said and done, then, the free expression of sexual matter can be suppressed and some people branded criminals and imprisoned, *in order to protect other people from themselves.*

One fascinating aspect of this "weak, uninformed, unsuspecting, gullible" rationale: it is not an idea which surfaced for the first time in *Paris Adult Theater* or the obscenity cases generally. The reader will recall, for example, that in *Virginia State Board of Pharmacy*, pharmacists could publish their prices only because the poor, sick and aged would benefit. Indeed, the needs of the allegedly helpless have long served as the justification for all sorts of other anti-individual rights legislation.

Burger took great pains to remind his dissenting liberal colleagues of just that.

The voting lineup in both *Miller* and *Paris* was identical. Chief Justice Burger wrote the majority opinion, joined by Justices Blackmun, Powell, Rehnquist (all Nixon appointees, "conservatives") and White (a Kennedy appointee, a "middle-of-the-roader"). Arch-

---

* *Paris Adult Theater I* v. *Slayton*, 413 U.S. 49, 64, 93 S.Ct. 2607, 2638-2639 (1973); emphasis added.

liberal Douglas dissented in a separate opinion; Justice Brennan also dissented in a separate opinion, joined by Justices Marshall (like Brennan, a liberal) and Stewart (a "middle-of-the-roader").

In Burger's majority opinion, he needled the dissenters about their seemingly new-found antipathy to government regulation. Burger's references to "state regulation of commercial and business affairs," to "federal securities and antitrust laws and a host of federal regulations," to protecting "the physical environment from pollution," to state "blue sky" laws for regulating "what sellers of securities may write or publish about their wares," to "constitutionally unchallenged laws" prohibiting certain consensual conduct, to regulating "public accommodations," and more, were not very subtle reminders to his dissenting colleagues that, in case after case, they had approved of government subordination of the individual to what *they* had perceived as society's greater needs. They too, Burger chided them, had pulled at the need-over-rights oars. Twice, he reminded the dissenters explicitly:

> Understandably those who entertain an absolutist view of the First Amendment find it uncomfortable to explain why rights of association, speech, and press should be severely restrained in the marketplace of goods and money, but not in the marketplace of pornography.
>
> * * *
>
> States are told by some that they must await a "laissez-faire" market solution to the obscenity-pornography problem, paradoxically "by people who have never otherwise had a kind word to say for laissez-faire," particularly in solving urban, commercial, and environmental pollution problems.[53]

If government control of the marketplace was sauce for the liberal geese, Burger was asking, why wasn't government control of certain forms of expression sauce for the liberal ganders? Why, indeed? The Chief Justice's point was unanswerable. The same anti-individual rights values which the liberals had employed, over conservative opposition, to control individuals in the marketplace, now allowed conservatives, over liberal opposition, to control individuals in the realm of ideas.

The principal point that emerges from all this is clear: an anti-individual rights premise makes it possible—indeed, inevitable—for government to control us in all ways and at all times because the premise knows no difference between issues. Indeed, it knows no difference between justices, all of whom hold it as a basic tenet.

The Brennan and Douglas dissents in *Paris* and *Miller* dramatically demonstrate this fact. Though the Court appeared to be narrowly divided in both cases, the division existed only on a pragmatic level, not in principle.

In *Paris*, Brennan renounced the offspring he had conceived in *Roth*, nurtured in *Memoirs*, and raised through more than thirty other obscenity cases:

> I am forced to conclude that the concept of "obscenity" cannot be defined with sufficient specificity and clarity to provide fair notice to persons who create and distribute sexually oriented materials, to prevent substantial erosion of protected speech as a byproduct of the attempt to suppress unprotected speech, and to avoid very costly institutional harms.[54]

But Brennan's belated recognition of the practical problem associated with obscenity was only that: a recognition, *not* that suppression of obscenity was wrong because it violated individual rights, but that *it did not work*. The following statement by Brennan says it all:

> That is not to say, of course, that a State must remain utterly indifferent to—and take no action bearing on—the morality of the community. The traditional description of state police power does embrace the regulation of morals as well as the health, safety, and general welfare of the citizenry. See, e.g., *Village of Euclid* v. *Ambler Realty Co.* [!]. . . . And much legislation—compulsory public education laws, civil rights laws, even the abolition of capital punishment—is grounded at least in part, on a concern with the morality of the community.[55]

Brennan's belief that the will of the collective community could vest in government the power to regulate morality, that *in principle* the suppression of obscenity was an acceptable government activity (though in practice it simply did not work) was hardly a ringing endorsement of individual rights.

Neither, unfortunately, was Douglas's dissent. As strange as it may seem, Douglas opposed the particular suppression of obscenity in *Miller* and *Paris*, on the one hand, while on the other, he explicitly endorsed the principle of suppression. Opposed to the California and Georgia laws which made the suppression there possible, Douglas nevertheless unequivocally suggested how the thread of altruism-collectivism-statism could *permanently* be woven into our constitutional fabric:

> We deal here with a regime of censorship which, if adopted, should be done by *constitutional amendment* after full debate by the people. If a constitutional amendment authorized censorship, the censor would probably be an administrative agency. Then criminal prosecutions could follow as, if, and when publishers defied the censor and sold their literature.
>
> * * *
>
> *If there are to be restraints on what is obscene, then a constitutional amendment should be the way of achieving the end.* There are societies where religion and mathematics are the only free segments. It would be a dark day for America if that were our destiny. *But the people can make it such if they choose to write obscenity into the Constitution and define it.*
>
> If it is to be defined, let the people debate and decide by a constitutional amendment what they want to ban as obscene and what standards they want the legislatures and the courts to apply. Perhaps the people will decide that the path towards a mature, integrated society requires that all ideas competing for acceptance must have no censor. Perhaps they will decide otherwise.[56]

With this shocking statement, Justice William O. Douglas, probably the Supreme Court's all-time arch-liberal, coolly asserted that should enough people want to repeal the First Amendment, they have the right to do so. If principle is to be sacrificed, he is saying, let it be via a numbers game. A decision by a Court of nine justices, and presumably a law passed by 500-plus Members of Congress, is an objectionable route to censorship. But let three-quarters of the states join in, and somehow, by thus increasing the number of violators, an egregious violation of rights becomes acceptable.

With friends like Douglas, the cause of individual rights needs no enemies—a point brought home dramatically in the next chapter's companion topic to sexual expression: actual sexual conduct.

6.

SEX

*Defend me from my friends; I can defend myself from
my enemies.*
                        —Claude Louis Hector Villars

Several years ago *The New York Times* carried a fascinating story
from Bombay by respected journalist Henry Kamm. Entitled "India
State is Leader in Forced Sterilization," the article reported that:

> An Indian state with a population of 50 million has become the first
> political entity in the world to legislate population control by forced
> sterilization.
>
> *   *   *
>
> [The law] requires that men up to age 55 and women up to 45 be
> sterilized within 180 days of the birth of their third living child. The
> measure puts the first obligation on men, and affects women only if their
> husbands are exempt because vasectomy would endanger their lives.
>
> *   *   *
>
> The measure provides prison terms of up to two years for those who
> fail to be sterilized. Dr. Pai [Bombay's Director of Family Planning]
> said that in practice offenders would be sterilized and paroled.
>
> *   *   *
>
> He accused the Roman Catholic Church of disregarding the growing

disproportion between population growth and the availability of resources to sustain it. Society, he said, has a duty to act against "people pollution" just as it removes latrines that are built on a river used by people.*

Equally fascinating was another *Times* report which appeared about four weeks later. This one, from Vientiane, was entitled "Laos Bans Birth Control to Build Population After a Decade of War." The article stated that:

> The Laotian government has banned birth control. The decision to outlaw the use of contraceptives throughout Laos, perhaps the first nation to be subjected to such an action, is designed, according to government officials, to build up the nation's population, decimated by more than a decade of war and more than a year of flight of a sizeable part of the population into exile . . . .
>
> *   *   *
>
> In a recent interview, the Information Minister, Sisana Sisane, observed that "there is so much empty land in Laos" that a larger population was needed to develop it.†

With Indian men being forcibly stripped of their reproductive capacity, and Laotian women being forced to reproduce, the obvious common denominator in their treatment was force. A superficial difference between what happened in the two countries is that in socialist India the force was initiated by democratically elected legislators out to *limit* population while in communist Laos, unelected party functionaries initiated force in order to *increase* population.

Common to India's compulsory sterilization program and Laos's forced reproduction program is the need-over-rights doctrine that is undercutting our own country—even in the seemingly private domain of sex. Should the spectacle of statist India spay/neutering its hapless citizens and statist Laos making studs and brood mares out of theirs, tempt American skeptics to insist "It can't happen here!", let them read on.

---

* *The New York Times*, August 13, 1976.
† *The New York Times*, September 9, 1976.

It seems safe to say that the traditional attitudes of American culture make monogamous heterosexual marriage the moral norm, and all expression of sexuality outside that institution morally deviant. [Footnote omitted.] The American states possess a battery of criminal statutes whose overall design, if not effect, appears to be to confine all interpersonal sexuality to marriage. [Footnote omitted.] Although it is not considered immoral to remain unmarried, the unmarried person who has coitus with another single person is guilty of fornication under the statutes of a number of states. If he or she engages in intercourse with a married person, one or both of them may also have committed the crime of adultery. In either situation if the partners engage in any form of genital stimulation other than coitus, they may violate the various criminal statutes prohibiting "unnatural" sex acts. These same statutes are almost invariably violated by any form of homosexual activity. If any partner pays the other for his sexual favors, the crimes of prostitution and patronizing a prostitute may have been committed. And if the two individuals are within certain degrees of kinship to one another, they could be guilty of incest. In a number of states, unmarried people who desire contraceptives for the prevention of pregnancy [once found] themselves . . . barred by law from obtaining them for such purposes. [Footnote omitted.] [Until 1973, women deprived of contraceptives who conceived became criminals if they aborted.] Even if no evidence of sexual connection is present, a male and female who live together without the benefit of marriage can be prosecuted for illicit cohabitation.*

A close examination of each statist restraint on sex and sexually related conduct—fornication, adultery, "sodomy" (which covers a multitude of "sins"), prostitution, incest, contraception, abortion, cohabitation—would reveal that such restraints are rooted, often explicitly, in the altruist-collectivist ethics. An examination of that kind, however, would quickly become cumulative rather than enlightening. To prove the thesis, it is necessary only to survey three representative categories: sodomy, contraception, and abortion.

On the subject of male homosexuality, the Old Testament does not mince words, commanding that: "Thou shalt not lie with mankind, as

---

* Walter Barnett, *Sexual Freedom and the Constitution: An Inquiry into the Constitutionality of Repressive Sex Laws* (University of New Mexico Press, Albuquerque, 1973) pp. 1-2.

with womankind; it is abomination."* "If a man lie with mankind, as with womankind, both of them have committed abomination: they shall surely be put to death; their blood shall be upon them."[†]

Over the next millennia or two, prohibitions against homosexuality, and noncoital sexual conduct generally, were considerably broadened:

> Sodomy historically and medically refers to anal intercourse, or buggery, but the statutes on sodomy include all manner of sexual activity conceived by someone, somewhere, at one time or another, to be "unnatural"; and this means, of course, in this sexually repressed society almost every variety of sexual activity other than "natural" coitus. Sodomy laws thus cover, in one state or another, not only buggery, but fellatio (oral-genital contact with the female), homosexual behavior . . . and even mutual masturbation.[‡]

The states of Arizona, Virginia and Washington offer some interesting contemporary examples of sodomy laws.

In Arizona:

> A person who wilfully commits, in any *unnatural* manner, any lewd or lascivious act upon or with the body or any part or member thereof of a male or female person, with the intent of arousing, appealing to or gratifying the lust, passion or sexual desires of either of such persons, is guilty of a felony.**

While Virginia's law, unlike Arizona's, does not use the word "unnatural," the same idea is unmistakably conveyed in its title: "Crimes against nature." In Virginia:

> "If any person shall carnally know in any manner . . . any male or female person by the anus or by or with the mouth, or voluntarily submit to such carnal knowledge, he or she shall be guilty of a felony. . . ."[††]

---

* Leviticus 18:22.

† Leviticus 20:13.

‡ Hugh M. Hefner, "The Legal Enforcement of Morality," 40 *Univ. of Colorado Law Review* 199, 210 (1968).

** Arizona Revised Statutes, 13-652, as amended; emphasis added.

†† Virginia Code Annotated Section 18.1-212, as amended.

In a virtually identical statute, Washington gets a bit more specific anatomically:

> "Every person who shall carnally know in any manner . . . any male or female person by the anus or with the mouth or tongue; or who shall voluntarily submit to such carnal knowledge . . . shall be guilty of sodomy."*

These criminal laws, punishing—often severely—various forms of sodomy, could be multiplied many times over. Even in the 1980s, virtually every state in America has one.

Virtually every state has had one throughout our nation's history. Yet the United States Supreme Court has had little to say about antisodomy laws *directly*. Indirectly, the Court has made abundantly clear that it does not disapprove of them—as will become obvious following a brief but necessary digression.

The jurisdiction of the Supreme Court is "discretionary," meaning that it only hears cases it is willing to review.

There are two ways to get a case before the Supreme Court. One is to request a "Writ of Certiorari" (a Latin term meaning a Court order by which the Supreme Court agrees to take, hear, and probably decide, a lower court case).

The other way is to "appeal" to the Supreme Court "as a matter of right"—a procedure applicable to certain kinds of lower court cases, allowed by law to come before the Court *automatically*.

There is no contradiction between, on the one hand, the Court's jurisdiction being "discretionary," and, on the other, having some cases come before it "automatically." As we shall see, the Court fully controls which "automatic" cases it will, and will not, decide.

The certiorari jurisdiction of the Supreme Court has been invoked countless times by people who ran afoul of antisodomy laws. Each time, despite the nature of the offense and the often severe punishment, the Court has denied certiorari. The result: the lower court's conviction, and harsh sentence, is left standing.

Keith Milton Rhinehart is a case in point. He was charged with sodomy in the State of Washington "in that he 'did carnally know one

---

* Revised Code of Washington 9.79.100.

James Guy Miller, a living human being and a male person, with the mouth and tongue; * * * ' "¹ Since it made no difference under the Washington law that the sex act had been consensual, Rhinehart was convicted. One of his contentions, on appealing to the state's highest court, was that the statute was "unconstitutional in that it purports to make criminal, private consensual acts which are not affected with sufficient public interest to be the subject of the exercise of the police power of the state."² The Supreme Court of Washington responded to this argument: "There is no merit to this contention. The legislature has, by this enactment, considered the public interest served by it."³

In other words, the statute was constitutional and Rhinehart's conviction valid because, on the subject of sodomy, the people of Washington had spoken.

This theme was somewhat expanded in the court's answer to Rhinehart's final contention: that the sodomy statute violated the Constitution's religion clause "in that, those persons who hold a majority belief have imposed their ethics on others who follow homosexual practices."* As far as it went, that argument took a pretty good aim at the altruist-collectivist premises that had inspired Washington's antisodomy law in the first place, and then gotten Rhinehart convicted and punished simply for indulging in his sexual preference. The court, relying on a religion case decided by the Supreme Court of the United States back in 1890 (also rooted in ethics), responded to this argument:

> With man's relations to his Maker and the obligations he may think they impose, and the manner in which an expression shall be made by him of his belief on those subjects, no interference can be permitted, *provided always the laws of society, designed to secure* its peace and prosperity, and *the morals of its people*, are not interfered with.†

It is worth noting that the court, in disposing of Rhinehart's religion argument, *expressly* relied on *Reynolds* v. *United States*, the polygamy

---

* *State* v. *Rhinehart*, 424 P.2d 906, 910 (1967). It is noteworthy that Rhinehart realized Washington's antisodomy laws were rooted in ethics. It is unfortunate that he was unable to lay bare what those ethics really were.

† *State* v. *Rhinehart*, 424 P.2d 906, 910 (Wash. 1967), quoting *Davis* v. *Beason*, 133 U.S. 333, 342, 10 S.Ct. 299, 300 (1890); emphasis added.

case discussed in Chapter 4. One bad precedent inevitably leads to another.

In sum, the Supreme Court of Washington upheld Rhinehart's conviction for consensual fellatio because it considered society's moral values, at least by Washington's standards, preferable to Rhinehart's.

Rhinehart became a "criminal." He faced a prison sentence. The Supreme Court of the United States, on October 9, 1967, unanimously denied Rhinehart's Petition for a Writ of Certiorari.[4]

Eleven years later, in 1976, the case of *Doe* v. *Commonwealth's Attorney*[5] fared no better via the "automatic appeal" route.

Homosexuals had attacked Virginia's "crimes against nature" law in the federal district court. Each plaintiff charged that, as a male homosexual, he was in danger of being prosecuted for violating Virginia's antisodomy law, and that the law was unconstitutional when "applied to his active and regular homosexual relations with another *adult male, consensually* and *in private.*"*

Initially taking the safe route of the uncommitted, the United States District Court for the Eastern District of Virginia stated: "[n]o judgment is made upon the wisdom or policy of the statute."[6] Nevertheless, by a 2-1 vote, the court upheld the constitutionality of the law.† There were four reasons.

First, nosecounting: "Many states have long had, and still have, statutes and decisional law criminalizing conduct depicted in the Virginia legislation."[7]

Second, venerableness: "Although a questionable law is not removed from question by the lapse of any prescriptive period, the longevity of the Virginia statute does testify to the State's interest and its legitimacy. It is not an upstart notion; it has ancestry going back to Judaic and Christian law. [Citing Leviticus 18:22 and 20:13] * * * In sum, we believe that the sodomy statute, so long in force in Virginia,

---

* *Doe* v. *Commonwealth's Attorney*, 403 F.Supp. 1199, 1200 (1975); emphasis in original.

† The dissenting judge, though contending that "[p]rivate consensual sex acts between adults are matters, absent evidence that they are harmful, in which the state has no legitimate interest" (*Doe* v. *Commonwealth's Attorney*, 403 F.Supp. 1199, 1203 (1975)), also believed that "the promotion of morality and decency" by the state was a "salutary" legislative goal." *Doe* v. *Commonwealth's Attorney*, 403 F.Supp. 1199, 1205 (1975).

has a rational basis of State interest demonstrably legitimate . . . ."[8]

Third, normalcy: There existed "no authoritative judicial bar to the proscription of homosexuality—since it is obviously no portion of marriage, home or family life . . . ."[9]

Fourth, *moral values*: " . . . to sustain its action, the State is not required to show that moral delinquency actually results from homosexuality. It is enough for upholding the legislation to establish that the [homosexual] conduct is likely to end in a contribution to moral delinquency."[10] And in the same vein, drawing on the earlier case of *Poe* v. *Ullman* in the Supreme Court, which we shall encounter later in this chapter: " . . . I would not suggest that *adultery, homosexuality, fornication and incest are immune* from criminal inquiry, *however privately practiced*. So much has been explicitly recognized in acknowledging the State's rightful concern for its people's moral welfare . . . . * * * If a State determines that punishment [for homosexuality], even when committed in the home, is appropriate in the promotion of morality and decency, it is not for the courts to say that the State is not free to do so."*

The Virginia plaintiffs-homosexuals appealed the lower court's decision—a direct appeal to the United States Supreme Court (as they had a *statutory right* to do). Before briefs were even filed, the Commonwealth's Attorney (in a routine maneuver) told the Supreme Court that the lower court's decision was so manifestly correct it should be affirmed without further ado—recommending, in effect, that the plaintiffs have no opportunity to argue their case or file a brief.

The Supreme Court obliged, affirming the lower court decision and denying the plaintiffs their day in court. In so doing, the Court gave its imprimatur to the principle enunciated by the lower court (and by hundreds of other courts through the years): the sexual conduct of consenting adult homosexuals could be subordinated to the moral values of the rest of society. It was as if the United States Supreme Court were saying about all these antisodomy statutes that were transforming sexual "deviants" into criminals: full speed ahead! Homosexuals were not the only ones sacrificed to the prevailing moral code. So were even monogamously married heterosexuals—especially when *their* values clashed with religious values.

---

* *Doe* v. *Commonwealth's Attorney*, 403 F.Supp. 1199, 1202 (1975); emphasis in original.

In a 1968 lecture at the Ford Hall Forum in Boston, entitled "Of Living Death,"* Ayn Rand identified the basic antisexual premises of the then-recent Papal Encyclical "Humanae Vitae" ("Of Human Life"):

> For centuries, the dominant teaching of the church held that sexuality is evil, that only the need to avoid the extinction of the human species grants sex the status of a *necessary* evil and, therefore, only procreation can redeem or excuse it. In modern times, many Catholic writers have denied that such is the church's view. But what *is* its view? They did not answer.
>
> Let us see if we can find the answer in the encyclical "*Humanae Vitae.*"
>
> Dealing with the subject of birth control, the encyclical prohibits all forms of contraception (except the so-called "rhythm method"). The prohibition is total, rigid, unequivocal. It is enunciated as a moral absolute.
>
> Bear in mind what this subject entails. Try to hold an image of horror spread across space and time—across the entire globe and through all the centuries—the image of parents chained, like beasts of burden, to the physical needs of a growing brood of children—young parents aging prematurely while fighting a losing battle against starvation—the skeletal hordes of unwanted children born without a chance to live—the unwed mothers slaughtered in the unsanitary dens of incompetent abortionists—the silent terror hanging for every couple, over every moment of love. If one holds this image while hearing that this nightmare is not to be stopped, the first question one will ask is: Why? In the name of humanity, one will assume that some inconceivable, but crucially important reason must motivate any human being who would seek to let that carnage go on uncontested. †

Rand found the answer she was seeking in the pages of the Papal Encyclical itself. But three years before the Encyclical, the secular equivalent to that answer was spelled out by the United States Supreme Court in *Griswold* v. *Connecticut*.[11]

At stake was the constitutionality of two Connecticut anticontraceptive statutes:

---

* The lecture appears in the September, October, and November 1968 issues of *The Objectivist*.

† Ayn Rand, "Of Living Death" (*The Objectivist*, September 1968), p. 1.

Any person who uses any drug, medicinal article or instrument for the purpose of preventing conception shall be fined not less than fifty dollars or imprisoned not less than sixty days nor more than one year or be both fined and imprisoned.[12]

* * *

Any person who assists, abets, counsels, causes, hires or commands another to commit any offense may be prosecuted and punished as if he were the principal offender.[13]

Estelle T. Griswold was Executive Director of the Planned Parenthood League of Connecticut. Dr. Buxton, a licensed physician and a professor at the Yale Medical School, served as the League's Medical Director at its Center in New Haven.

Both Mrs. Griswold and Dr. Buxton each "gave information, instruction, and medical advice to *married persons* as to the means of preventing conception. They examined the wife and prescribed the best contraceptive device or material for her use. Fees were usually charged, although some couples were serviced free."*

Mrs. Griswold and Dr. Buxton were arrested, charged as accessories to their clients' crime (using contraceptives), and found guilty. Their convictions were affirmed, first by an appeals court in Connecticut, then by that state's highest court.

The United States Supreme Court reversed the convictions. But— and it is a profoundly important "but"—the *Griswold* decision is a mass of contradictory reasoning, from its multiple concurring opinions to its multiple dissents. And worse: the decision as a whole stands as testament to government's power to regulate morality.

Justice Douglas spoke for the majority.† But in his zeal to legalize the use of contraceptives by married persons, he constructed out of whole cloth a previously unheard-of constitutional "right of privacy." And in the process, he clearly implied that, while he disapproved of outlawing the *use* of contraceptives (as in Connecticut), he might well rule *constitutional* a law regulating the "manufacture or sale"[14] of contraceptives!

The Goldberg-Warren-Brennan concurring opinion concluded that Connecticut's anticontraceptive statute was unconstitutional—but

---

* *Griswold* v. *Connecticut*, 381 U.S. 479, 480, 85 S.Ct. 1678, 1679 (1965); emphasis in original.

† Justice Goldberg wrote a concurring opinion, in which Justices Warren and Brennan joined.

not because of some amorphous, ill-defined "right of privacy." Their rationale, instead, was based on an amorphous, ill-defined, concept of "fundamental rights."

The fact that the three concurring justices voted against the statute is outweighed by the altruist-collectivist premises they revealed in the process—the very premises which made the Connecticut statute possible in the first place. Said Goldberg:

> In determining which rights are fundamental, judges are not left at large to decide cases in light of *their* personal and private notions. Rather, they must look to the "*traditions* and [*collective*] *conscience* of our people" to determine whether a principle is "so rooted [there] * * * as to be ranked as fundamental." . . . *

A modest disclaimer. But while confessing that a judge's values are not the litmus paper by which "fundamental rights" are revealed, Goldberg openly defers to "the traditions and [collective] conscience of our people"—an admission that rights are neither absolute nor anchored in the Constitution: rights are whatever society decides they are. Goldberg further incriminates himself by his view of what *Connecticut* society had already "decided" in related areas of sexual conduct:

> The State of Connecticut does have statutes, *the constitutionality of which is beyond doubt*, which prohibit *adultery* and *fornication*. . . .
>
> * * *
>
> Finally, it should be said of the Court's holding today that it in no way interferes with a State's *proper* regulation of sexual promiscuity or misconduct.†

Goldberg, Warren, and Brennan were, of course, motivated by altruism-collectivism-statism—principles about as controllable as a loose cannon on a rolling deck. How else to explain why they denied Connecticut the power to interfere with use of contraceptives (by married persons), while simultaneously *granting* it the power to interfere with adultery, fornication, sexual promiscuity and "miscon-

---

* *Griswold* v. *Connecticut*, 381 U.S. 479, 493, 85 S.Ct. 1678, 1686 (1965); emphasis added.

† *Griswold* v. *Connecticut*, 381 U.S. 479, 498-499, 85 S.Ct. 1678, 1689 (1965); emphasis added.

duct"? How else to explain why, with the following words, they *implicitly* endorsed a forced sterilization program for married persons:

> . . . the Government, *absent a showing of a compelling subordinate state interest*, could not decree that all husbands and wives must be sterilized after two children have been born to them.*

So much for "fundamental rights."

Justice Harlan's concurring opinion was cast in the same mold, although Harlan's constitutional litmus paper was neither "right of privacy" nor "fundamental rights." In his view, "basic values 'implicit in the concept of ordered liberty' "[15] rendered Connecticut's anticontraception statute unconstitutional. Like his colleagues, Harlan embraced, in other respects, the very principles which made the Connecticut statute possible.† He started out, at least, by grasping the underlying issue:

> Precisely what is involved here is this: the State is asserting the right to enforce *its moral judgment* by intruding upon the most intimate details of the marital relation with the full power of the criminal law.‡

But in addressing himself to an argument that statutes barring (as immoral) the use of contraceptives were based on an "irrational" premise, and that such statutes subjected people "in a very important matter to the arbitrary whim of the legislature, and that it does so for no good purpose. . . . ,"[16] Harlan bared his collectivist soul:

> Yet the very inclusion of the category of morality among state concerns indicates that society is not limited in its objects only to the physical well-being of the community, but has traditionally concerned itself with *the moral soundness of its people* as well. Indeed to attempt a line between public behavior and that which is purely consensual or solitary would be to withdraw from community concern a range of subjects with which every society in civilized times has found it

---

* *Griswold* v. *Connecticut*, 381 U.S. 479, 496-497, 85 S.Ct. 1678, 1688 (1965); emphasis added.
† Harlan's belief that Connecticut's anticontraception law violated "basic values 'implicit in the concept of ordered liberty' " was based on "reasons stated at length in [his] dissenting opinion in *Poe* v. *Ullman*," 367 U.S. 497, 81 S.Ct. 1752 (1961). Harlan's quotations below are from that dissent.
‡ *Poe* v. *Ullman*, 367 U.S. 497, 548, 81 S.Ct. 1752, 1779 (1961); emphasis added.

necessary to deal. The laws regarding marriage which provide both
when the sexual powers may be used and the legal and societal context
in which children are born and brought up, as well as laws forbidding
adultery, fornication and homosexual practices which express the
negative of the proposition, *confining sexuality to lawful marriage*,
form a pattern so deeply pressed into the substance of our social life that
any Constitutional doctrine in this area must build upon that basis . . . *

Though the order in which Harlan made his points was a bit
convoluted, what he was saying was not. Harlan was saying that any
attempt to isolate in people's lives an area of purely *private* conduct, is
necessarily to infringe on areas where society has long had its own
interests. Translation: don't try to draw a line between your "private"
activities and those over which society may claim an interest—no
clear distinction exists.

Harlan was saying that tradition justifies society's concern "with
the moral soundness of *its* people."† Harlan was saying that society
rightly manifests that concern through marriage laws regulating
"when the sexual powers may be used," and "laws forbidding
adultery, fornication and homosexual practices" which confine
"sexuality to lawful marriage."

Harlan, clearly enamored of this theme—the state's power to
regulate morality—could not resist restating it:

> The right of privacy most manifestly is not an absolute. Thus, I would
> not suggest that adultery, homosexuality, fornication and incest are
> immune from criminal enquiry, however privately practiced. *So much
> has been explicitly recognized in acknowledging the State's rightful
> concern for its people's moral welfare.*
>
> *   *   *
>
> Adultery, homosexuality and the like are sexual intimacies which
> the State forbids altogether, but the intimacy of husband and wife is
> necessarily an essential and *accepted* feature of the institution of
> marriage, an institution which the State must not only allow, but which
> always and in every age it has fostered and protected.
>
> *   *   *
>
> . . . requiring husband and wife to render account before a criminal

---

* *Poe* v. *Ullman*, 367 U.S. 497, 545-546, 81 S.Ct. 1752, 1778 (1961); emphasis added.

† Emphasis added.

tribunal of their uses of that intimacy, is surely a very different thing indeed from punishing those who establish *intimacies which the law has always forbidden and which can have no claim to social protection.**

In view of the troublesome constitutional guarantee that neither life, liberty, nor property shall be deprived without "due process of law," however, Harlan apparently felt compelled to "justify" himself:

> Due process has not been reduced to any formula; its content cannot be determined by reference to any code. The best that can be said is that through the course of this Court's decisions it has represented the *balance* which our Nation, built upon postulates of respect for the liberty of the individual, has struck *between* that *liberty and the demands of organized society.*†

There it is, again: the blind belief that whenever individual liberty clashes with society's demands, a *balance* somehow can be struck between the two; the blind refusal to recognize that America's constitutional history is littered with the casualties of government's doomed attempts at an impossible balancing act.

Justice White wrote his own concurring opinion, voting to invalidate the Connecticut statute. But he, too, agreed that Connecticut's "policy against all forms of promiscuous or illicit sexual relationships, be they premarital or extramarital, [was] concededly a permissible and legitimate legislative goal."[17]

Justices Black and Stewart both dissented, not because they agreed with Connecticut's anticontraceptive law *personally*, (they opposed it), but because they saw no way the Supreme Court could strike it down—not without a *specific* provision of the Constitution they could literally point to. Perhaps a provision which read: Congress shall make no law interfering with a person's right to use contraceptives! And, once again, both dissents echoed the sentiments of their concurring brethren: that government possesses the power to regulate sexual morality and, presumably, morality in general.

The fact that *Griswold* v. *Connecticut* is popularly considered a

---

* *Poe* v. *Ullman*, 367 U.S. 497, 552-553, 81 S.Ct. 1752, 1782 (1961); emphasis added.
† *Poe* v. *Ullman*, 367 U.S. 497, 542, 81 S.Ct. 1752, 1776 (1961); emphasis added.

victory for individual rights is due to a combination of misinformation, context-dropping, and wishful thinking. *Griswold* constitutes a mish-mash of altruism-collectivism-statism at its worst and most revealing.

Eight years later, another case would understandably receive the same popular accolade as *Griswold*—based on the same misconception. The case was *Roe v. Wade*; the issue: abortion.

A Texas statute, like those in a majority of the states, had outlawed abortion except to save the mother's life. Jane Roe (a pseudonym), unmarried and pregnant, sued in a federal court to declare the Texas antiabortion statute unconstitutional. Relying principally on the *Griswold* case and the Fourteenth Amendment's concept of "due process," Roe claimed that the statutes abridged her right of personal privacy and her right to personal liberty. She cited no other source, constitutional or otherwise, in defense of her right to an abortion.

The Supreme Court's decision in *Roe* was, to say the least, fragmented—even more than *Griswold*'s had been. (Of the nine Supreme Court justices, six wrote separate opinions. The majority opinion was written by Justice Blackmun and concurred in by Chief Justice Burger, Justices Douglas, Brennan, Stewart, Marshall, and Powell. Three of the concurring justices—Burger, Douglas and Stewart—wrote their own individual opinions. While Justice Rehnquist joined in a dissent by Justice White, he wrote a separate dissenting opinion of his own.)

In his majority opinion, Blackmun ruled the Texas antiabortion statute unconstitutional. How did he reach that momentous decision?

First, by canvassing a wide variety of sources; he was seeking their attitudes about abortion. He examined ancient views concerning abortion, but they proved inconclusive. He discovered that the Hippocratic Oath's rigid antiabortion stand had been unpopular even at the time it was formulated.* He examined English common law and hit pay dirt: apparently, even under the early statutes, abortion to save the mother's life was not considered a criminal act. According to Blackmun, "abortion performed *before* 'quickening'—the first recognizable movement of the fetus *in utero*, appearing usually from the

---

* L. Edelstein, *The Hippocratic Oath* 10 (1943); see *Roe v. Wade*, 410 U.S. 113, 93 S.Ct. 705, 715 (footnote) (1973).

16th to the 18th week of pregnancy—was not an indictable offense."*
Blackmun discovered further that in those days, even abortion of a
quick fetus had not been a felony—merely a lesser offense; that,
though the "quickening" distinction once existed in England, it had
vanished in 1837, reappeared in 1861, and remained until 1967, when
the law was greatly liberalized. Blackmun did not fare as well in his
survey of American law. He found that it had followed the pre-existing
English common law's "quickening" distinction only until mid-
nineteenth century—after which the distinction gradually began to
disappear until "[b]y the end of the 1950s, a large majority of the
jurisdictions banned abortion, however and whenever performed,
unless done to save or preserve the life of the mother."[18]

Summarizing his survey of the past, Blackmun observed:

> It is thus apparent that at common law, at the time of the adoption of
> our Constitution, and throughout the major portion of the 19th century,
> abortion was viewed with less disfavor than under most American
> statutes currently [1973] in effect. Phrasing it another way, a woman
> enjoyed a substantially broader right to terminate a pregnancy than she
> does in most States today. At least with respect to the early stage of
> pregnancy, and very possibly without such a limitation, the opportunity
> to make this choice was present in this country well into the 19th
> century. Even later, the law continued for some time to treat less
> punitively an abortion procured in early pregnancy.[19]

Next, Blackmun turned his attention to medical views, past and
prevailing. The American Medical Association, since mid-nineteenth
century, had bitterly condemned abortion, only to ameliorate its harsh
view in the mid-1960s. More pay dirt. In reviewing the American
Public Health Association's pro-abortion position, he noted that just
the year before, the American Bar Association had approved a
Uniform Abortion Act prepared by the prestigious Conference of
Commissioners on Uniform State Laws. Blackmun's potpourri of
current views now included legal as well as medical.

What was Blackmun seeking from all this opinion-gathering? Some
kind of justification. If, historically, abortion had received equivocal
treatment, the Court's task—coming up with a favorable abortion

---

* *Roe v. Wade*, 410 U.S. 113, 132, 93 S.Ct. 705, 716 (1973); emphasis in original.

ruling—would be easier; the justices could write, as it were, on a clean slate. What they wrote was, in turn, equivocal:

> We, therefore, conclude that the right of personal privacy includes the abortion decision, but that this right is *not unqualified* and must be considered against *important state interests* in regulation.*

The Court had before it a case going to the heart of so fundamental a personal choice that one might have expected to find a United States Supreme Court opinion that was a dazzling array of legal/constitutional arguments [they did exist], adorned with impeccable reasoning and irrefutable logic. We find, instead, as *sole* constitutional justification for its decision, the amorphous, Douglas-invented "right of personal privacy" borrowed from *Griswold*.

Even Blackmun had to concede that "privacy" was nowhere to be found in the Constitution. So, following Douglas's earlier lead, he tried to weave a "privacy" pattern into the Bill of Rights by borrowing threads where he could. Even so, Blackmun's entire fifty-four-page opinion—which would invalidate antiabortion laws nationwide—contained a *single* paragraph devoted to the constitutional basis for the Court's conclusion:

> The Constitution does not explicitly mention any right of privacy. In a line of decisions, however, going back perhaps as far as ... 1891 ... the Court has recognized that a right of personal privacy, or a guarantee of certain areas or zones of privacy, does exist under the Constitution. In varying contexts, the Court or individual Justices have, indeed, found at least the roots of that right in the First Amendment ... in the Fourth and Fifth Amendments ... in the penumbras of the Bill of Rights ... in the Ninth Amendment ... or in the concept of liberty guaranteed by the first section of the Fourteenth Amendment ... These decisions make it clear that only personal rights that can be deemed "fundamental" or "implicit in the concept of ordered liberty" ... are included in this guarantee of personal privacy. They also make it clear that the right has some extension to activities relating to marriage ... procreation ... contraception ... family relationships ... and child rearing and education. ... [20]

---

* *Roe* v. *Wade*, 410 U.S. 113, 154, 93 S.Ct. 705, 727 (1973); emphasis added.

Blackmun's constitutional pastiche spawned reactions from two of his colleagues; both are instructive.

Justice Stewart, in his concurring opinion, flatly rejected the "right of privacy" rationale:

> There is no [federal] constitutional right of privacy, as such. "[The Fourth] Amendment protects individual privacy against certain kinds of governmental intrusion, but its protections go further, and often have nothing to do with privacy at all. Other provisions of the Constitution protect personal privacy from other forms of governmental invasion. But the protection of a person's *general* right to privacy—his right to be let alone by other people—is, like the protection of his property and of his very life, left largely to the law of the individual states."*

Stewart believed the Texas antiabortion statute should be tested and found wanting—but by a standard with more substance: "Several decisions of this Court make clear that freedom of personal choice in matters of marriage and family is one of the liberties protected by the Due Process Clause of the Fourteenth Amendment."[21]

Justice Rehnquist also flatly rejected the "right of privacy" rationale, underscoring, in dissent, that the majority opinion lacked a constitutional foundation:

> I have difficulty in concluding . . . that the right of "privacy" is involved in this case. Texas . . . bars the performance of a medical abortion by a licensed physician on a plaintiff such as [Jane] Roe. A transaction resulting in an operation such as this is not "private" in the ordinary usage of that word. Nor is the "privacy" that the Court finds here even a distant relative of the freedom from searches and seizures protected by the Fourth Amendment . . . which the Court has referred to as embodying a right to privacy.
>
> If the Court means by the term "privacy" no more than that the claim of a person to be free from unwanted state regulation of consensual transactions may be a form of "liberty" protected by the Fourteenth Amendment, there is no doubt that similar claims have been upheld in our earlier decisions on the basis of that liberty. * * * But that liberty is not guaranteed absolutely against deprivation, only against depriva-

---

* *Roe* v. *Wade*, 410 U.S. 133, 168, 93 S.Ct. 705, 734 (footnote); emphasis in original.

tion without due process of law. *The test traditionally applied in the area of social and economic legislation is whether or not a law such as that challenged has a rational relation to a valid state objective.* [Citing a Supreme Court case, *Williamson* v. *Lee Optical Co.,* authored by *Douglas.*]*

Rehnquist and Stewart had made the same telling points: there was no such thing as a *Griswold-Roe* "right of privacy;" the antiabortion laws should have been tested by the usual due process/liberty standard: whether the legislation had a rational relation to a valid state objective.

Although Rehnquist parted company with Stewart on what constituted a valid state objective, and both justices parted company with the majority on the correct constitutional test to be applied, every justice on the Bench agreed that under no circumstances, did a woman have an *absolute* right to an abortion. Always, there were other factors to be considered. What did society feel about abortion? What important state interests were at stake? Indeed, when the technical aspects and the historical review that make up the bulk of Blackmun's majority opinion are pared away, virtually all that remains is a preoccupation with state interests:

> . . . a State may properly assert important interests in safeguarding health, in maintaining medical standards, and in protecting potential life. At some point in pregnancy, these respective interests become sufficiently compelling to sustain regulation of the factors that govern the abortion decision.[22]

And the particular state interest that seemed to interest Blackmun most, judging from the frequency with which it was mentioned in his opinion, was the state's "important and legitimate interest in preserving and protecting the health of the pregnant woman."[23]

Arch-liberal Douglas agreed—in spades: "While childbirth endangers the lives of some women, voluntary abortion at any time and place regardless of medical standards would impinge on a rightful concern of society. The woman's health is part of that concern; as is the life of the fetus after quickening."[24] From whence comes this

---

* *Roe* v. *Wade*, 410 U.S. 113, 172-173, 93 S.Ct. 705, 736-737 (1973); emphasis added.

seemingly unchallengeable absolute? Why is society's interest strongly asserted, never explained, and deemed to require not even a modicum of proof? Doubtless, Douglas and his brethren were operating on the basic premise of *Muller* v. *Oregon*, that solidly liberal decision, with its Hitlerian overtones: " . . . as healthy mothers are essential to vigorous offspring, the physical well-being of woman becomes an object of public interest and care in order to preserve the strength and vigor of the race."*

A necessary corollary of avowed state interest in the pregnant woman is state interest in her unborn child—an interest Blackmun could hardly ignore. The Court made a series of findings: "the word 'person,' as used in the Fourteenth Amendment, does not include the unborn,"[25] "the unborn have never been recognized in the law as persons in the whole sense,"[26] [we do not] "resolve the difficult question of when life begins."[27] But the "potential life" issue had yet to be dealt with. Blackmun "dealt" with it in two sentences: "[T]he State's important and legitimate interest in potential life is at viability. *This is so because the fetus then presumably has the capability of meaningful life outside the mother's womb.*"†

On the basis of such specious and almost offhand "reasoning," the Supreme Court of the United States came up with the following mixed bag:

Because the Court judged abortions within the first trimester to be as medically safe (in 1973) as, or even safer than, normal childbirth, abortions in the first three months of pregnancy "must be left to the medical judgment of the pregnant [woman and her] attending physician."[28]

Because the Court assumed a state interest in the health of the pregnant woman, abortions during "the stage subsequent to approximately the end of the first trimester" could be regulated "in ways that are reasonably related to maternal health"[29] (e.g., licensed physicians, adequate facilities).

Because the Court asserted a state interest in potential life, "[f]or

---

* *Muller* v. *Oregon*, 208 U.S. 412, 421, 28 S.Ct. 324, 326 (1908). Indeed, the *Roe* Court's explicit endorsement of the state's interest in "the preservation and protection of maternal health" (*Roe* v. *Wade*, 410 U.S. 113, 163, 93 S.Ct. 705, 732 (1973)) clearly echoes *Muller*.

† *Roe* v. *Wade*, 410 U.S. 113, 163, 93 S.Ct. 705, 732 (1973); emphasis added.

the stage subsequent to viability [approximately during the final trimester], the state . . . may, if it chooses, regulate, and even proscribe, abortion except where it is necessary, in appropriate medical judgment, for the preservation of the life or health of the mother."[30]

Perhaps because too many Americans have come to think of their rights as conditional, and themselves as less than wholly free, it was to be expected that *Roe* v. *Wade* would be greeted as a victory not just for women's rights, but for individual rights as well. Perhaps a small— even pyhrric—victory in a long, losing war assumes significance. Perhaps most people have lost sight of the fact that rights flow, not from accommodation, compromise or "balancing," but from defensible moral principle. Whatever the reasons, the Supreme Court's abortion decision is regarded, by friend and foe, as a giant liberalizing step forward. In a practical sense and in the short run, the cause of free-choice abortion *has* been advanced; women *can* abort—at least for now. But in principle and over the long run, the cause of freedom has been pushed a giant step backward.

Few people realize that *Roe* v. *Wade* opened a Pandora's Box when the Supreme Court legitimized a "state interest" in pregnant women and their unborn children. This time around—in *this* case—antiabortion laws have been struck down and some women permitted to have abortions. Next time around—in some future case—antiabortion laws may be upheld and *no* women permitted to have abortions. The time after next—depending on the current "state interest"—women may even be *compelled* to abort. A farfetched notion? Science fiction? Not if we accept the ultimate logic of *Roe* v. *Wade*—as seen from the perspective of a 1977 Supreme Court case.

The states, in the wake of *Roe* v. *Wade*, had to revise not only their abortion laws, but also a considerable number of related laws which were directly and indirectly affected by that decision, such as criminal laws and Medicaid (which, prior to *Roe* v. *Wade*, had funded certain childbearing expenses).

Connecticut Welfare Department regulations, which paid for childbirth expenses, limited state Medicaid benefits for first trimester abortions to those which were "medically necessary." So in 1977 the Supreme Court was asked to decide "whether the Constitution requires a . . . State to pay for . . . [non-medically necessary] abortions when it pays for childbirth."[31] In other words, did Connecticut have a constitutional right to a Medicaid funding policy which treated birth and abortion differently?

Before answering that question, the Court felt obliged to point out what *Roe* v. *Wade* had *not* held: "*Roe* did not declare an unqualified 'constitutional right to an abortion' . . . . * * * It implies no limitation on the authority of a State to make a value judgment *favoring childbirth over abortion*, and to implement that judgment by the allocation of public funds."[32]

Presumably, then, "[it] implies no limitation on the authority of the State to make a value judgment favoring "abortion over childbirth."

The Court in *Maher*, like the State of Connecticut, clearly favored childbirth over abortion. But following the 6-3 majority's statement that "[t]he State unquestionably has a 'strong and legitimate interest in encouraging normal childbirth', . . . an interest honored over the centuries," there appeared a footnote as astonishing as it was ominous:

> In addition to the direct interest in protecting the fetus, a State may have *legitimate demographic concerns about its rate of population growth*. Such concerns are basic to the future of the State and in some circumstances could constitute a substantial reason for departure from a position of neutrality between abortion and childbirth.*

How reminiscent of that democratic Indian state whose "demographic concerns about its rate of population growth" prompted it to depart "from a position of neutrality between abortion and childbirth"— by a program of forced sterilization.

Three members of the Court dissented in *Maher*, two of them the Court's remaining "liberals." One might have expected a ringing denunciation from Brennan and Marshall of the majority's naked assertion that, should population grow too large or food become too scarce, society could forcibly dump the unborn.

No denunciation was forthcoming.

---

* *Maher* v. *Roe*, 432 U.S. 464, 478, 97 S.Ct. 2376, 2385 (footnote) (1977); emphasis added.

7.

SLAVERY

All slavery has its origin in power, and is against right.

—John McLean, Associate Justice,
Supreme Court of the United States

The cases already discussed in this book have demonstrated the extent to which altruism and collectivism have dominated our system at the expense of rights. How, through repressive legislation, society's needs, as perceived by government, have been implemented at great sacrifice to the individual.

However, even those cases—spanning the subjects of business, property, contracts, religion, speech and sex—do not tell the whole story of just how extreme that sacrifice has been. The remaining five cases do.

As we have seen in Chapter 6, *Roe* v. *Wade*, decided in 1973, stands for the proposition that government possesses substantial power over whether a pregnant woman must deliver or whether she may abort; an outrageous interference with individual rights. Yet, in a case decided nearly half a century before *Roe*, the Supreme Court had already invaded this sensitive, highly personal area, with this result: government has the power to prevent a woman from even *becoming* pregnant.[1]

Seventeen-year-old Carrie Buck allegedly was:

> . . . a feeble-minded white woman who was committed to the State [mental hospital]. She [was] the daughter of a feeble-minded mother in the same institution, and the mother of an illegitimate feeble-minded child.[2]

A Virginia statute back in the 1920s provided that the health of certain types of individuals, and the welfare of society generally, could be promoted by the sterilization of mental defectives. Carrie Buck was ordered sterilized, Virginia having found that she was "the probably potential parent of *socially inadequate* offspring, likewise afflicted, that she may be sexually sterilized without detriment to her general health and that her welfare and that of society will be promoted by *her sterilization*."* The Virginia Supreme Court upheld the statute, observing that it "was not meant to punish but to protect the class of socially inadequate citizens from themselves and to *promote the welfare of society by mitigating race degeneracy and raising the average standard of intelligence of the people of the state*."†

Eventually, the question of the Virginia law's constitutionality reached the United States Supreme Court. While the opinion of the legendary Justice Oliver Wendell Holmes for an 8-1 Court contained some familiar ideas and minced no words, those words still have the power to shock:

> We have seen more than once that the public welfare may call upon the best citizen for their lives. It would be strange if it could not call upon *those who already sap the strength of the State* for these *lesser sacrifices*, often not felt to be such by those concerned, in order to prevent our being swamped with incompetence. It is *better for all the world*, if instead of waiting to execute degenerate offspring for crime, or to let them starve for their imbecility, *society can prevent those who are*

---

* *Buck* v. *Bell*, 274 U.S. 200, 207, 47 S.Ct. 584, 585 (1927); emphasis added.

† *Buck* v. *Bell*, 143 Va. 310, 130 S.E. 516, 519 (1925); emphasis added.

manifestly unfit from continuing their kind. The principle that sustains compulsory vaccination is broad enough to cover cutting the Fallopian tubes . . . .Three generations of imbeciles are enough.*

The underlying principles in which the Court's opinion is rooted— represented by concepts like "public welfare," "sacrifices," "better for all the world," "society"—should, by now, require no elaboration. But the idea worth pursuing here is that in the name of those principles, in the name of avoiding socially inadequate offspring, promoting society's welfare, mitigating race degeneracy, raising the average intelligence of Virginians, and not sapping the strength of the state, a woman's procreative capacity was extinguished by state mandated and state executed sterilization.

So was that of some 8,299 other persons who were involuntarily sterilized in Virginia between 1924 and 1972. So were some 65,000 persons throughout America in the first half of this century.

In Virginia, deceit played a role; some of those sterilized were told that an appendectomy or other comparable operation was being performed. Some victims were merely retarded. Some, according to Dr. K. Ray Nelson (now Director of Lynchburg, Virginia's and America's largest institution for the retarded), "would not be admitted to this institution today."†

Carrie Buck was one of them. Her sister Doris was another. The sister, at age seventeen, had been involuntarily sterilized, then told she had undergone an appendectomy. According to Dr. Nelson, Doris Buck, who is alive today, and married, "was not particularly retarded."‡ According to the *Times*:

> For years, [Dr. Nelson] said, she and her husband . . . could not understand why she could not bear children. "This is one of the tragedies," Dr. Nelson said. He said the statistical probability of their having a retarded child was no greater than for the general population.
>
> "I broke down and cried," [she] told the [newspaper]. "My husband and me wanted children desperate—we were crazy about them. I never

---

* *Buck* v. *Bell*, 274 U.S. 200, 205, 47 S.Ct. 584, 585 (1927); emphasis added.

† *The New York Times*, February 23, 1980.

‡ *The New York Times*, February 23, 1980.

knew what they done to me."*

Doris Buck did not seem consoled by the knowledge that her "lesser sacrifice," (a barren life) had been made for the "welfare of society . . . and [to] rais[e] the average intelligence of the people of the state."

Her sister Carrie fared worse, in a way; she had been used. The Virginia physician who started the state's sterilization program in 1924 considered Lynchburg "a cleaning house," existing to "give these young women education, industrial and moral training, sterilize them and send them out to earn their own living."† Facing litigation over previous sterilizations, the physician needed a test case—judicial sanction to legitimize his work in eugenics. Carrie Buck was his guinea pig, the alleged linchpin in "[t]hree generations of imbeciles." (What would Justice Holmes do, one wonders, with the fact that Carrie Buck, alive as recently as 1980 and living in abject poverty in Virginia, had led a reasonably normal life for half a century, as did her sister, Doris, and that Carrie Buck's daughter, whom Virginia authorities had characterized as "slow" and whom Holmes and his Court had characterized as an "imbecile," had actually been considered a "bright child" by her second-grade teachers?)

Carrie Buck was sterilized, although Holmes's assumption of hereditary imbecility, which surely would be challenged today, was open to serious doubt even in 1924.

Lest optimists write off these tragic and fearsome examples of altruism-collectivism-statism run amok as regrettable ancient history, they should know that *today* fully half of the states in America (including Virginia), still have laws on their books allowing for the involuntary sterilization of "incompetents." Not only has *Buck* v. *Bell* not been overruled, but fifteen years after it was decided the Supreme Court pointedly declined an invitation to do so. Instead, the Court did just the opposite, resurrecting the principles upon which *Buck* v. *Bell* rested.

The case was *Skinner* v. *Oklahoma*,[3] involving that state's Habitual Criminal Sterilization Act. Assuming that certain "criminal

---

* *The New York Times*, February 23, 1980.

† *The New York Times*, February 23, 1980.

tendencies" were transmissible genetically (how is that for a *literally* collectivist judgment?), the Act provided that "habitual criminals"* were to be sterilized if the procedure could be accomplished "without detriment to his or her general health."

The Oklahoma act was struck down by the Supreme Court. Although Justice Jackson observed, "[t]here are limits to the extent to which a legislatively represented majority may conduct biological experiments at the expense of the dignity and personality and natural powers of a minority—even those who have been guilty of what the majority define as crimes,"[4] the act was not held unconstitutional for this reason. What the Court disapproved of was Oklahoma's arbitrary classification of which criminal acts were "moral turpitude" felonies and which were not, since this would result in an arbitrarily administered sterilization program. Indeed, Douglas's opinion for a unanimous Court, as well as the two concurring opinions (by Chief Justice Stone and Justice Jackson [the Chief Prosecutor at Nuremberg!]) clearly implied that not all involuntary sterilization laws were unconstitutional. Stone went so far as to agree that:

> Undoubtedly a state may, after appropriate inquiry, constitutionally interfere with the personal liberty of the individual to prevent the transmission by inheritance of his socially injurious tendencies. [citing] *Buck* v. *Bell* . . . .[13]

Buck and *Skinner* make clear that the Supreme Court has openly and consistently endorsed the states' power to involuntarily sterilize certain individuals. No comfort can be found in the fact that, so far, government has approved sterilization programs for so-called mental defectives and habitual criminals. The important, inescapable point is not how far these sterilization statutes have gone, but that they *exist* and have been *upheld*. Given the anti-individual rights attitudes that have wormed their way into the core of America's political-legal system, there can be no doubt that such laws are a time bomb waiting to be detonated by any number of potential fuses.

---

* An habitual criminal was one who, having been convicted two or more times for crimes "amounting to felonies involving moral turpitude" either in an Oklahoma court or in a court of any other state, was thereafter convicted of such felony in Oklahoma and was sentenced to a term of imprisonment in an Oklahoma penal institution.

The "legitimate demographic concerns" of *Maher* v. *Roe* could well be one.

In February, 1980, *The New York Times* reported what might be another:

OFFICIAL URGES STERILIZATION
OF TEXAS WELFARE RECIPIENTS

Austin, Tex., February 27 (UPI)—The chairman of the agency that administers welfare programs in Texas said today that welfare recipients should have mandatory sterilizations or abortions to avoid having children they cannot afford.

Hilmar G. Moore, chairman of the Board of Human Resources and Mayor of Richmond, also suggested that welfare recipients, including children, be required to work in order to receive government aid.

In light of *Griswold*, *Roe*, *Maher*, *Buck*, and *Skinner*, Chairman Moore's "suggestion" cannot be viewed as mere hyperbole.

As to Moore's advocacy of forced labor, the Supreme Court addressed that issue as long ago as 1916, and the people affected were not even on the government dole.

Years ago, Florida had a law providing that:

Every able-bodied male person over the age of twenty-one years, and under the age of forty-five years . . . shall be . . . required to work on the roads and bridges of the . . . counties for six days of not less than ten hours each in each year when summoned to do so . . . .*

The statute also provided that such an "able-bodied male person" could produce an able-bodied substitute in his place or buy his way out. Failure to discharge one's yearly manual labor responsibility to the State of Florida was a crime—a misdemeanor, punishable by fine or imprisonment.

Jake Butler "was convicted in the county judge's court, Columbia County, upon a charge of failing to work on a road, and sentenced to jail for thirty days."[6] When his case reached the United States

---

* Chapter 6537, Laws of Florida (Acts of 1913, pp. 469, et seq.).

Supreme Court, its opinion was written for a *unanimous* Bench by arch-conservative Justice McReynolds (who would later so forcefully and eloquently dissent in "property" cases like *Euclid* v. *Ambler Realty Co.* (zoning) and the *Gold Clause Cases* (contract)).

To Jake Butler's claims that forced labor on county roads constituted involuntary servitude in violation of the antislavery Thirteenth Amendment, and deprived him of liberty and property in violation of the due process guarantee of the Fourteenth Amendment, McReynolds answered:

> In view of *ancient usage* and the *unanimity* of judicial opinion, it must be taken as settled that, unless restrained by some constitutional limitation, a state has inherent power to require every able-bodied man within its jurisdiction to labor for a reasonable time on public roads near his residence without direct compensation. This is a part of the *duty* which he owed to the *public*.*

So, based on how things were done in other lands and long ago, based also on the unanimous consensus of unnamed courts, our Supreme Court held that public needs justified forcing free American citizens to toil like convicts—unless the Constitution forbade it. Of course, the Court was unable to find any such constitutional provision. But what of the constitutional prohibition of involuntary servitude? What of the due process clause, which protects our liberty and our property? The Thirteenth Amendment's proscription of involuntary servitude, asserted the Court, was inapplicable; it was intended to apply only to African-type slavery, not "to interdict enforcement of those duties which individuals owe to the State, such as services in the army, militia . . . ."[7] Nor was due process of any help to Butler because requiring "work on the public roads has never been regarded as a deprivation of either liberty or property."[8]

Involuntary sterilization. Forced labor. It is hard to conceive of worse outrages than these occurring in America. But worse has occurred, as this book's last three cases dramatically prove.

The day after the sneak attack on American forces at Pearl Harbor, the United States declared war on Japan. Soon after, events began to

---

* *Butler* v. *Perry*, 240 U.S. 328, 330, 36 S.Ct. 258 (1916); emphasis added.

occur which, when they ended in the Supreme Court of the United States three years later, would leave America much less free than before.

February 19, 1942: President Roosevelt issued Executive Order No. 9066.[9] Avowedly designed to protect the country against espionage and sabotage, the order allowed certain military commanders to establish military zones in the United States "from which any or all persons may be excluded, and with respect to which, the right of any person to enter, remain in, or leave shall be subject to whatever restrictions" the "Military Commander may impose in his discretion."

The next day: Lieutenant General DeWitt was designated Military Commander of the Western Defense Command, which embraced the westernmost states of the country (about one-fourth of the total area of the nation).

March 2, 1942 (about ten days later): General DeWitt announced Public Proclamation No. 1,[10] which recited that the entire Pacific Coast was "particularly subject to attack, to attempted invasion * * * and, in connection therewith, is subject to espionage and acts of sabotage." The Proclamation further stated that "as a matter of military necessity" General DeWitt was establishing Military Areas Nos. 1 and 2, and that "[s]uch persons or classes of persons as the situation may require" would, by later orders, "be excluded from all of Military Area No. 1" and from certain specified zones in Military Area No. 2. The Areas embraced California, Washington, Oregon, Idaho, Montana, Nevada, Utah, and southern Arizona. The various orders required that if anyone of Japanese, German, or Italian ancestry (including American citizens!) residing in Military Area No. 1 wanted to change their residence, a Change of Residence Notice had to be filed with the authorities.

March 2, 1942: Toyosaburo Korematsu knew, since San Leandro, California, was within Military Area No. 1, that he was in the following position: though his parents had been born in Japan, *he* had been born here, and under the Constitution he was an American citizen; Roosevelt had authorized the military to exclude him from certain areas, and prevent him from entering or leaving them without permission; his home town was in Military Area No. 1; General DeWitt would soon exclude him from where he lived.

March 21, 1942: Congress passed a law making it a misdemeanor to "enter, remain in, leave, or commit any act in any military area or military zone" contrary to the Military Commander's orders.[11]

March 24, 1942: General DeWitt ordered a curfew (later to be upheld by the Supreme Court) and began issuing exclusion orders relating to specified areas. At that time Korematsu himself had not yet been excluded.

March 29, 1942: Proclamation (No. 4)[12] effectively "froze" Korematsu in Military Area No. 1, by prohibiting anyone from exiting it, pending future orders.

May 3, 1942: General DeWitt issued a Civilian Exclusion Order (No. 34).[13] It provided that after May 8, 1942, all persons of Japanese ancestry—noncitizens and citizens alike—were to be excluded from a certain zone in Military Area No. 1. The zone embraced the place where Korematsu lived.

As Justice Roberts would later explain in his *Korematsu v. United States* dissent:[14]

> The order required a responsible member of each family and each individual living alone to report, at a time set, at a Civil Control Station for instructions to go to an Assembly Center, and added that any person failing to comply with the provisions of the order who was found in the described area after the date set would be liable to prosecution under the Act of March 21, 1942 . . . . It is important to note that the order, by its express terms, had no application to persons within the bounds "of an established Assembly Center pursuant to instructions from this Headquarters * * * ." The obvious purpose of the orders made, taken together, was to drive all citizens of Japanese ancestry into Assembly Centers within the zones of their residence, under pain of criminal prosecution.
>
> The predicament in which [Korematsu] thus found himself was this: he was forbidden . . . to leave the zone in which he lived; he was forbidden . . . to be found within that zone unless he were in an Assembly Center located in that zone. General DeWitt's report to the Secretary of War concerning the programme of evacuation and relocation of Japanese makes it entirely clear . . . that an Assembly Center was a euphemism for a prison. No person within such a center was permitted to leave except by Military Order.
>
> In the dilemma that he dare not remain in his home, or voluntarily leave the area, without incurring criminal penalties, and that the only way he could avoid criminal punishment was to go to an Assembly

Center and submit himself to military imprisonment, [Korematsu] did nothing.

As a result, Korematsu was indicted in a federal court, charged with knowingly remaining within the area covered by General DeWitt's Exclusion Order. Convicted, Korematsu received a suspended sentence and five years probation. Doubtless, the sentence was "lenient" because, as Justice Roberts reported, Korematsu

> ... was at once taken into military custody and lodged in an Assembly Center. We further know that [a few months earlier] the President had promulgated [an] Executive Order ... establishing the War Relocation Authority under which so-called Relocation Centers [mostly in the Arizona desert] ... were established ... and that [Korematsu] has been confined either in an Assembly Center ... or has been removed to a Relocation Center .... [15]

Against this factual background, the Supreme Court was called upon to decide the constitutionality of Korematsu's exclusion. In an opinion written by Justice Black, concurred in by arch-liberal Douglas and others, the Court upheld the exclusion.

Why?

The Court was quick to concede that most Japanese-Americans "were loyal to this country." [16] Black wrote:

> ... hardships are part of war, and war is an aggregate of hardships. All citizens alike, both in and out of uniform, feel the impact of war in greater or lesser measure. Citizenship has its responsibilities as well as its privileges, and in time of war the burden is always heavier. Compulsory exclusion of large groups of citizens from their homes, except under circumstances of direst emergency and peril, is inconsistent with our basic institutions. But when under conditions of modern warfare our shores are threatened by hostile forces, the power to protect must be commensurate with the threatened danger. [17]
>
> * * *
>
> To cast this case into outlines of racial prejudice, without reference to the real military dangers which were presented, merely confuses the issue. Korematsu was not excluded from the Military Area because of hostility to him or to his race. He was excluded because the properly constituted military authorities feared an invasion of our West Coast

and felt constrained to take proper security measures, because they decided that the military urgency of the situation demanded that all citizens of Japanese ancestry be segregated from the West Coast temporarily, and finally, because Congress, reposing its confidence in this time of war in our military leaders—as inevitably it must— determined that they should have the power to do just this. There was evidence of disloyalty on the part of some, the military authorities considered that the need for action was great, and time was short.[18]

In short, Korematsu was excluded simply because the government had decided that his exclusion was *necessary*.

Black's attitude in *Korematsu* is illuminated by two statements he made after the decision. Professor Gerald T. Dunne reports that:

> A decade later [Black] uncompromisingly defended what he did [in his *Korematsu* opinion]—"The President could have declared martial law. Instead, they took the better way of passing a law to detain them. There's a difference between war and peace. You can't fight a war with the courts in control". And the racial aspects of the case, he insisted, were there only because "a particular race was the threatening invader."*

"Another decade later," Professor Dunne reveals, Black "was even more adamant" about his *Korematsu* opinion:

> I would do precisely the same thing today, in any part of the country. I would probably issue the same order were I President. We had a situation where we were at war. People were rightly fearful of the Japanese in Los Angeles, many loyal to the United States, many undoubtedly not, having dual citizenship—lots of them.
>
> *They all look alike to a person not a Jap.* Had they [the Japanese] attacked our shores you'd have a large number fighting with the Japanese troops. And a lot of innocent Japanese-Americans would have been shot in the panic. Under these circumstances I saw nothing wrong with moving them away from the danger area.†

To sum up the prevailing attitude both on and off the Bench: Most

---

* Gerald T. Dunne, *Hugo Black and the Judicial Revolution* (Simon and Schuster, 1977), p. 213.

† Gerald T. Dunne, *Hugo Black and the Judicial Revolution* (Simon and Schuster, 1977), p. 213; emphasis added.

Japanese-Americans were loyal. Some may not have been. They all "looked alike." We faced a "military necessity" (born of a palpably absurd invasion threat, which would have required the enemy to maintain a 5,000-mile-long ocean supply line from Japan to the West Coast). Our government regarded the country's peace of mind as an important value. Korematsu's exclusion, therefore, is constitutional. By a 6-3 vote of our Supreme Court, it was so ordained.

Though there were dissenters, it did not follow, as we have seen before, that there was disagreement on basic principles.

The *Korematsu* case was no different. Justice Roberts's dissent candidly characterized the places where Japanese-Americans were being detained as "concentration camps." Yet he did not challenge their existence. He quarreled only with the *extent* and *permanence* of the forced exclusion, not with the government's *power* to exclude. Indeed, Roberts concluded that "[t]he liberty of every American citizen freely to come and to go must frequently, in the face of sudden danger, be temporarily limited or suspended."[19]

Justice Murphy, in his dissent, disapproved of the exclusion because it "goes over 'the very brink of constitutional power' and falls into the ugly abyss of racism."[20] Yet Murphy's basic quarrel was with the facts: he saw no significant military necessity for the exclusion. And like Roberts, he accepted the principle that the end sometimes justifies the means:

> The judicial test of whether the Government, on a plea of military necessity, can validly deprive an individual of any of his constitutional rights is whether the deprivation is reasonably related to public danger that is so "immediate, imminent, and impending" as not to admit of delay and not to permit the intervention of ordinary constitutional processes to alleviate the danger.[21]

So while Murphy deplored "the ugly abyss of racism," he was willing, under certain circumstances, to sanction it.

That the exclusion of Korematsu and the thousands of other Japanese-Americans was, in large part, racially motivated can be seen from General DeWitt's own report of the evacuation,* which refers to

---

* Final Report, Japanese Evacuation from the West Coast, 1942, by Lt. Gen. J.L. DeWitt. Dated June 5, 1943, the Report was not made public until January 1944.

all persons of Japanese ancestry as "subversive," as members of "an enemy race" whose "racial strains are undiluted," and as constituting "over 112,000 potential enemies ∗ ∗ ∗ at large today" along the Pacific coast. Testifying on April 13, 1943, before the House of Representatives Naval Affairs Subcommittee to Investigate Congested Areas, DeWitt frankly admitted:

> I don't want any of them here. There is no way to determine their loyalty. The West Coast contains too many vital installations essential to the defense of the country to allow any Japanese on this coast. ∗ ∗ ∗ The danger of the Japanese was, and is now—if they are permitted to come back—espionage and sabotage. It makes no difference whether he is an American citizen, he is still a Japanese. American citizenship does not necessarily determine loyalty. ∗ ∗ ∗ But we must worry about the Japanese all the time until he is wiped off the map.*

How ironic that Japan did not subjugate us militarily in World War II, leaving our basic freedoms intact, while our own government undermined them by sacrificing the individual rights of some citizens to the racist fears of others. Racism, as Ayn Rand has pointed out:

> . . . is the lowest, most crudely primitive form of collectivism. It is the notion of ascribing moral, social or political significance to a man's genetic lineage—the notion that a man's intellectual and characterological traits are produced and transmitted by his internal body chemistry. Which means, in practice, that man is to be judged, not by his own character and actions, but by the characters and actions of a collective of ancestors.†

In 1942, Japanese-Americans on the West Coast were objects of more than racial hatred. Fear and envy of their productiveness and the wish not to compete with them was widespread. Justice Murphy took note of it in a footnote to his dissenting opinion:

> Special interest groups were extremely active in applying pressure for mass evacuation. See House Report No. 2124 (77th Cong., 2d

---

* Part 3, pp. 739-740 (78th Cong., 1st Sess.).

† Ayn Rand, "Racism," *The Virtue of Selfishness* (The New American Library, 1965), p. 172.

Sess.) 154-6; McWilliams, Prejudice, 126-8 (1944). Mr. Austin E. Anson, managing secretary of the Salinas Vegetable Grower-Shipper Association, has frankly admitted that "We're charged with wanting to get rid of the Japs for selfish reasons. We do. It's a question of whether the white man lives on the Pacific Coast or the brown man. They came into this valley to work, and they stayed to take over. * * * They undersell the white man in the markets. * * * They work their women and children while the white farmer has to pay wages for his help. If all the Japs were removed tomorrow, we'd never miss them in two weeks, because the white farmers can take over and produce everything the Jap grows. And we don't want them back when the war ends, either."[22]

So, added to the ranks of the Carrie and Doris Bucks, whose fertility was sacrificed to an experimental theory of eugenics, and the Jake Butlers, who became literal slaves to the roads and bridges society needed built, were Japanese-Americans whose alien race our society feared and whose productive ability it envied.

In wartime, unfortunately, legions of such victims are forced by that keeper of last resort, the government, to feed the ravenous appetite of societal need. In wartime, society needs able-bodied men. To get them, the government resorts to conscription.

To understand the extent to which government has truly become our keeper, it is necessary first to step backward into American constitutional history. The Declaration of Independence announced to the world that "[w]e hold these truths to be self-evident: that all men are created equal; that they are endowed, by their Creator, with certain unalienable rights, that among these are life, liberty and the pursuit of happiness. That to secure these rights, governments are instituted among men, deriving their just powers from the consent of the governed . . . "

As Ayn Rand has observed: "Whether one believes that man is the product of a Creator or of nature, the issue of man's origin does not alter the fact that he is an entity of a specific kind . . . and that rights are a necessary condition of his particular mode of survival."* The

---

* Ayn Rand, "Man's Rights," *The Virtue of Selfishness* (The New American Library, 1965), p. 126.

Declaration of Independence implicitly recognized this fact, affirming that man *has* the right to life and that government is created for the express purpose of protecting his rights.

The Declaration was a set of political principles. The Constitution of the United States was its practical implementation. But there were flaws in the Constitution—three in particular—which undermined it by contradicting the principle of unalienable rights. One was its failure to grant women the vote. Another was the compromise which condoned and institutionalized Negro slavery (a contradiction which ultimately exploded into the Civil War). The third was its failure to come to grips with the issue of conscription.

The American colonists were familiar with conscription, the Revolutionary War having been waged in part by men who were drafted pursuant to the constitutions of nine states. However, because they had been drafted only into *state* militia, the national government was forced, when it needed soldiers, to requisition them from the states. Some people deemed this arrangement inconvenient and sentiment arose for broader federal jurisdiction over military affairs.

When the Constitution was drawn up, the power of Congress to conscript was neither expressly denied nor granted. Article I, Section 8, spelled out certain general military powers. Congress was expressly given the power: "To declare War . . . To raise and support Armies . . . To provide and maintain a Navy . . . "

Just how sweeping were these war powers intended to be? The issue was not tested for nearly a century and a half, until World War I. On May 18, 1917, President Wilson signed into law the Selective Draft Act. It was intended to provide manpower to fight the trench warfare which had been draining the lifeblood of European countries for three years.

Ten men, who were indicted for failing to register under the Act, launched a broad-based constitutional attack against it—the first, and, until recent years, the last challenge of this kind ever made against the federal draft as such. (All subsequent legal challenges to conscription were of a more limited nature, designed to test or clarify particular provisions, such as the religious exemption clause and the law's alleged "inequality" for exempting women.)

Convicted in various federal district courts, the defendants finally reached the Supreme Court of the United States.[23] There, they raised several constitutional objections to the draft, all unsuccessfully. Though it is significant *that* the defendants lost in the Supreme Court (unanimously), much more significant is *how* the Court treated their constitutional arguments, and *why*.

One of the defendants' major arguments was that Congress lacked the power to enact a law forcing men to fight. The Court countered that the Constitution granted the power when it authorized Congress to declare war and to raise and support armies. "As the mind cannot conceive an army without the men to compose it," said the Court, "on the face of the Constitution the objection that it does not give power to provide for such men would seem to be too frivolous for further notice."[24]

At stake in these 1918 draft cases was an all-encompassing power to strip men of their personal liberty and send them out to die. At stake was whether men could be fined or jailed for refusing to lay their lives on the line for a cause which was not theirs. Yet the Court evaded the defendants' "Congressional power" argument, arbitrarily brushing it off as "too frivolous for further notice." This blatant refusal to address profound constitutional issues was a strategy which the Court was to employ consistently throughout the draft cases.

What the Court did, in attempting to dispose of the "Congressional power" argument, was to set up a false alternative: the government must either draft men, or do without an army. But a third choice had been suggested to the Court by the defendants: that Congress's delegated power to provide for an army should properly be interpreted as calling for volunteer enlistments. "This [said the Court] . . . challenges the existence of all power, for a governmental power which has no sanction to it and which therefore can only be exercised provided the citizen consents to its exertion is in no substantial sense a power."[25]

Give the government the power to do something, the Court was saying, and, *ipso facto*, it can use force. On that premise, the Constitution's delegation to Congress of the power to establish post offices would allow the government to draft postal employees, instead of hiring them like any other employer.

The defendants advanced still another argument: by reason of its religious exemption clauses (which allowed ministers and conscientious objectors to avoid the draft), the act violated the First Amendment's prohibition against government contributing to the establishment of religion. While there was merit to this argument—which it was the Court's duty to consider—once again, the Court skirted the issue: " . . . we pass without anything but statement . . . [this] proposition . . . because we think its unsoundness is too apparent to require us to do more."[26]

When the defendants addressed themselves to the Thirteenth Amendment—and cited as a bar to the draft its unequivocal prohibition of slavery and involuntary servitude—the Court again avoided a valid constitutional argument by declaring it "refuted by its mere statement." Avoidance was the safer course; it allowed the Court to ignore its own precedent in an earlier case: "While the immediate concern was with African slavery, the [Thirteenth] Amendment was not limited to that. It was a charter of universal freedom for all persons, of whatever race, color or estate, under the flag. * * * The plain intention was to abolish slavery of whatever name and form and all its badges and incidents; to render impossible any state of bondage; to make labor free, by prohibiting that control by which the personal service of one man is disposed of or coerced for another's benefit which is the essence of involuntary servitude."[27]

That was the Court's view in 1911. In the 1918 draft cases, however, that view had changed. Induction into the armed forces—involuntary servitude? Not at all, said the Court—not if some important duty to the state is involved:

> . . . as we are unable to conceive upon what theory the exaction by government from the citizen of the performance *of his supreme and noble duty* of contributing to the defense of the rights and honor of the nation, as the result of a war declared by the *great representative body of the people*, can be said to be the imposition of involuntary servitude . . . we are constrained to the conclusion that the contention to that effect is refuted by its mere statement.*

The defendants had anticipated this need-over-rights approach. In a groping, overgeneralized attempt to show that freedom and the draft were mutually exclusive, they argued, correctly, that compelled military service was "repugnant to a free government and in conflict

---

* *Selective Draft Law Cases*, 245 U.S. 366, 390, 38 S.Ct. 159, 165 (1918); emphasis added.

with all the great guarantees of the Constitution as to individual liberty. . . . ."[28] But they failed to support their argument by grounding it in a specific, fundamental constitutional provision.

The Court's answer amounted to a confession of its ethics and political philosophy: "But the premise of this proposition is so devoid of foundation that it leaves not even a shadow of ground upon which to base the conclusion. Let us see if this is not at once demonstrable. It may not be doubted that the very conception of a just government and its duty to the citizen includes the reciprocal obligation of the citizen to render military service in case of need and the right to compel it. . . . To do more than state the proposition is absolutely unnecessary. . . . "[29]

This naked endorsement of altruism-collectivism-statism was the work of nine justices who were unwilling to meet, and unable to discredit, one valid legal argument after another. There were, however, arguments of a *different* nature which the Supreme Court of the United States found persuasive—arguments it relied upon as "proof" for the proposition that the draft was constitutional.

Look, said the Court, at the " . . . practical illustration afforded by the almost universal legislation to that effect now in force."[30] Look, the Court was saying, at what *other* nations have done.

Thirty-three countries were cited in a footnote to the Court's opinion—thirty-three governments which, prior to 1918, had subjected their citizens to the draft: Argentina, Austria-Hungary, Belgium, Brazil, Bulgaria, Bolivia, Colombia, Chile, China, Denmark, Ecuador, France, Greece, Germany, Guatemala, Honduras, Italy, Japan, Mexico, Montenegro, Netherlands, Nicaragua, Norway, Peru, Portugal, Rumania, Russia, Serbia, Siam, Spain, Switzerland, Salvador, Turkey. The list includes every imaginable social and political system: monarchies and dictatorships; banana republics and primitive backwashes; brutal oriental despotisms and disjointed feudal kingdoms.

Missing from this list is a constitutional republic in which the government, created for the express purpose of protecting rights, derives its limited powers from the people.

Could our Supreme Court really have believed that American citizens were no more immune from statist force than the helpless peasants under the heel of the Russian Tsar, or the miserable serfs under the whip of Japanese feudal barons?

Could the Court have forgotten why so many immigrants "yearning to breathe free" fled to America's shores? To avoid conscription in their native countries!

Could the Court have forgotten that America was supposed to have been founded on the principle of inalienable rights, *not* on the antithetical doctrines which have plagued the rest of the world from the beginning of time?

Would the Court ignore its own earlier precedents: that in judging a law *our* Constitution and *our* form of government must be its only guide?

It could, and it did.

The Court's deplorable failure to think in principle contains one grim irony: included in its list of those countries which had draft laws—held up as an example for America to follow—was Germany, with which we were then at war.

In addition to taking an international popularity poll on the draft issue, the Court attempted to justify conscription on the basis of three periods of United States history: preconstitutional, the War of 1812, and the Civil War. To all three periods, it gave a dubious interpretation.

While in the preconstitutional period it had been the practice of the states to draft men into the militia, and while it was true that the states had thus set an unfortunate precedent at a critical time in our history, it did not follow—as the Court implied—that the Constitution transferred this arbitrary power from the states to the federal government. The Constitution speaks for itself: the federal government was given no explicit power to raise and support an army by means of a national *draft*. The grant of power was, at best, equivocal.

The War of 1812 was cited by the Court because James Monroe, then Secretary of War, had written to Congress recommending compulsory federal draft legislation. (Ironically, we were then at war with the British because they were impressing American seamen into their navy.) While the bill that was later introduced never passed, the Court implied that, but for the intervention of peace, the United States would have had a draft law at that time. In fact, there is ample evidence that the bill had faced an uncertain future in both houses of Congress.

In citing the Civil War period, the Court placed considerable emphasis on an 1863 conscription law, suggesting that it was good legal precedent to rely on. Not true. In the first place, the United States Supreme Court had never ruled on its constitutionality; the

Civil War Draft Act was never challenged beyond the highest court of Pennsylvania. Secondly, it provided for a financial alternative to the draft: draftees could find someone to take their place, or pay the Secretary of War up to three hundred dollars to find a substitute. (The essence of the Civil War Draft Act can thus be summed up as "your money or your life.") Thirdly, it expired *before* involuntary servitude had been outlawed by the Thirteenth Amendment, while the World War I draft law followed that Amendment.

Finally, the Supreme Court cited as authority a book entitled *The Law of Nations*, a classic work written by an eighteenth-century scholar-diplomat named Emmerich de Vattel. The Court's reference was understandably oblique. It would not do to quote from so revealing a political tract. Just *how* revealing can be gleaned from the following excerpt from Vattel's *The Law of Nations*:

> Every citizen is *bound to serve* and defend the State as far as he is able. *Society cannot otherwise be preserved*; and this union for the common defense is one of the first objects of all political association. Whoever is able to bear arms must take them up as soon as he is *ordered* to do so by the one who has the *power* to make war ... Since *every citizen or subject is obliged to serve the State*, the sovereign has the right, when the necessity arises, to conscript whom he pleases.*

Since society is only a number of individuals in a given geographical area, what Vattel, the Supreme Court, and the colonists who sanctioned state militias, really meant when they cried "the draft is necessary to preserve society," is: some men can be preserved only by *forcing* other men to preserve them.

And so the draft became yet another vehicle by which our government claimed countless victims. In the twentieth century alone, hundreds of thousands, from the Argonne Forest to the Vietnam jungles, have fallen in mute testimony to the consequences of altruism-collectivism-statism—victims not of powder and steel, but of ideas.

Conscription is evil. But while it is difficult to quantify degrees of evil with precision, one episode in our relatively brief history as a nation can claim the awful distinction of unparalleled evil.

---

* Emphasis added.

I refer to human slavery, which I characterized earlier in this book as "an utterly rightless status where one human being's very existence hangs on the slender thread of another's caprice."*

The Constitution of the United States, though marred by significant contradictions, was undeniably the first real charter of human liberty ever struck by man. Yet that obscene practice, slavery, was not abolished on the Constitutional Convention floor—as it should have been, no matter what the cost to the emerging nation.

The Constitution contains four related slavery provisions: the "three fifths of all 'other persons'" rule for apportioning taxes and Congressional representation;† the twenty-year bar before Congress could prohibit the "migration or importation of 'such persons' as any of the States . . . shall think proper to admit. . . . ";‡ the prohibition against eliminating the twenty-year ban by constitutional amendment;** and the provision that "[n]o person 'held to service or labour' in one state, under the laws thereof, escaping into another, shall, in consequence of any law or regulation therein, be discharged from service or labor, but shall be delivered up on claim of the party to whom such service or labour may be due."†† These four provisions explicitly recognized, and condoned, and assured the continuation of, so uncivilized a practice that it can rightly be called the epitome of statist tyranny. The American Constitution, then, set in motion forces which, more than once, nearly mortally wounded our nation, forces which have not yet fully come to rest.

Compromise always exacts its price. Out of the Constitutional Convention's compromise with slavery came, seventy years later, the infamous *Dred Scott* case.

Dred Scott was a Negro slave "owned" by an army doctor. Between 1834 and 1838 Scott and the doctor first resided in the slave state of Missouri, then in a free state and a free federal territory.

---

* The existence of slavery side by side with the founding of this country substantially undermined the achievement of the Founding Fathers.
† Art. I, Section 2.
‡ Art. I, Section 9.
** Art. V.
†† Art. IV, Section 2.

Eventually they returned to Missouri.

Scott's odyssey, though it arose in the ugly context of slavery, raised an interesting and important legal question: had he become free when taken into free territory? Scott thought that he had, and in 1846 began legal action to obtain his freedom. Eventually, his case reached the Supreme Court.

There were basically two related questions before the High Court. The first: whether Dred Scott was a citizen of Missouri and/or of the United States. The second: whether he had been freed by his sojourn to either a free state or a free territory.

Both questions were addressed by Chief Justice Roger B. Taney:

> The question is simply this: Can a negro, whose ancestors were imported into this country, and sold as slaves, become a member of the political community formed and brought into existence by the Constitution of the United States, and as such become entitled to all the rights, and privileges, and immunities, guaranteed by that instrument to the citizen? One of which is the privilege of suing in a court of the United States. . . . [31]

Sadly, Taney, answering for the Court majority, held:

> We think they are not, and that they are not included, and were not intended to be included, under the word 'citizens' in the Constitution, and can therefore claim none of the rights and privileges which that instrument provides for and secures to citizens of the United States. On the contrary, they were at that time considered as a subordinate and inferior class of beings, who had been subjugated by the dominant race, and, whether emancipated or not, yet remained subject to their authority, and had no rights or privileges but such as those who held the power and the Government might choose to grant them. [32]

To support his conclusion, Taney mustered a substantial body of evidence. Even a brief review of that evidence pains anyone who respects human dignity, but it does provide a rare glimpse of important pre-Civil War attitudes about slavery in America.

Taney began with a general historical observation about Negroes:

> It is difficult at this day to realize the state of public opinion in relation to that unfortunate race, which prevailed in the civilized and

enlightened portions of the world at the time of the Declaration of Independence [1776], and when the Constitution of the United States was framed and adopted [1787]. But the public history of every European nation displays it in a manner too plain to be mistaken.

They [Negroes] had for more than a century before been regarded as beings of an inferior order, and altogether unfit to associate with the white race, either in social or political relations; and so far inferior, that they had no rights which the white man was bound to respect; and that the Negro might justly and lawfully be reduced to slavery for his benefit. He was bought and sold, and treated as an ordinary article of merchandise and traffic, whenever a profit could be made by it. This opinion was at that time fixed and universal in the civilized portion of the white race. It was regarded as an axiom in morals as well as in politics, which no one thought of disputing, or supposed to be open to dispute; and men in every grade and position in society daily and habitually acted upon it in their private pursuits, as well as in matters of public concern, without doubting for a moment the correctness of this opinion.[33]

With this survey in place, Taney sketched out the workings and extent of the worldwide English slave trade, including its extension to the mother country's American colonies—which, when the Revolution began, had extensive legislation concerning slaves.

Next, the Chief Justice demonstrated that despite the seemingly universal language of the Declaration of Independence, it was mainfestly *not* intended to embrace the Negro slaves; nor were the Articles of Confederation. The Constitution itself, Taney pointed out, viewing slaves as a class apart, expressly intended to exclude them from state or federal citizenship.

Once the new government was formed, state laws continued to classify slaves separately. Indeed, as Taney observed:

The legislation of the States therefore shows, in a manner not to be mistaken, the inferior and subject condition of that race at the time the Constitution was adopted, and long afterwards, throughout the thirteen States by which that instrument was framed; and it is hardly consistent with the respect due to these States, to suppose that they regarded at that time, as fellow-citizens and members of the sovereignty, a class of beings whom they had thus stigmatized; whom, as we are bound, out of respect to the State sovereignties, to assume they had deemed it just and necessary thus to stigmatize, and upon whom they had impressed such deep and enduring marks of inferiority and degradation . . . .[34]

Taney went on to point out that even the new Congress, in its early legislation, had perpetuated the distinction between slaves and everyone else. That as late as 1820, the Charter for the City of Washington, D.C., reflected that distinction. That an 1821 opinion of the Attorney General of the United States and decisions of various state courts did likewise.

The evidence was substantial: Negro slaves were indeed a class apart, neither citizens of any state nor of the federal government.

Taney summed up his body of proof:

> We have the language of the Declaration of Independence and of the Articles of Confederation, in addition to the plain words of the Constitution itself; we have the legislation of the different States, before, about the time, and since, the Constitution was adopted; we have the legislation of Congress, from the time of its adoption to a recent period; and we have the constant and uniform action of the Executive Department, all concurring together, and leading to the same result. And if anything in relation to the construction of the Constitution can be regarded as settled, it is that which we now give to the word "citizen" and the word "people."[35]

As to the argument that Scott's sojourn into free jurisdictions had legally, if not literally, unchained him, Taney and the four southern associate justices saw Scott's claim as a once-in-a-lifetime opportunity: to extend slavery—legally—to *all* federal territory. One thing stood in their way: Congress's "Missouri Compromise." To understand why, some background information is necessary.

The Constitution provided that: "The Congress shall have power to dispose of and make all needful rules and regulations respecting the territory or other property belonging to the United States. . . . "*

When, in 1818, settlers in the territorial area of the lower Missouri river and the west bank of the Mississippi near St. Louis sought admission to the Union as the new State of Missouri, their proposed constitution permitted slavery. Many Americans were greatly opposed

---

* Art. IV, Section 3.

to the idea, and Congressional approval of Missouri's admission resulted in what, today, we would call a "package deal"—the infamous "Missouri Compromise." Maine was admitted as a free state. Missouri was admitted as a slave state. And Section 8 of the Missouri Enabling Act[36] *barred* slavery in *federal territory* north of a line drawn at 36° 30′ north latitude. By the Compromise, Congress maintained its power (apparently rooted in Article IV, Section 3 of the Constitution) to keep slavery out of all federal territories if it wished to do so. The Missouri Compromise also swept under the rug for another generation the issue of whether and where slavery would be extended.

That issue surfaced in *Dred Scott*, with Scott's "free territory" claim.

Taney, faced with the Missouri Compromise, which had *prohibited* slavery north of 36° 30′ north latitude, simply declared it unconstitutional!

The majority opinion held that while Congress did possess express constitutional power to govern federal territories (as in the Missouri Compromise), that power was limited to territories which had existed *prior* to the Constitution's adoption (in the late 1780s). Since the free territory north of 36° 30′ north latitude had been acquired much later, the Compromise's prohibition of slavery in that territory was deemed null and void.

Although Congress did possess power over "after acquired" territories, the source of that power, the Court went on to hold, was only implied—not expressed—in the Constitution. This being so, the exercise of that power—as with the Missouri Compromise's slavery prohibition—was subject to *express* constitutional limitations. Taney saw one such limitation as the sanctity of *"property."* In defense of it, he set forth the central thesis of the *Dred Scott* decision:

> . . . the rights of property are united with the rights of person, and placed on the same ground by the fifth amendment to the Constitution, which provides that no person shall be deprived of life, liberty, and property, without due process of law. An act of Congress which deprives a citizen of the United States of his liberty or property, merely because he came himself or brought his property into a particular Territory of the United States . . . could hardly be dignified with the name of due process of law.[37]

That was the Supreme Court's entire justification for allowing the practice of human slavery, an obscenely perverse interpretation of the fifth article of the *Bill of Rights*. What a turning inside-out of that venerable concept, "due process of law," with its origin in Magna Charta.

Taney had proved, all right, that Negroes were not (and were never intended to be) American citizens. His majority opinion had relegated Negroes, like inanimate objects, to the status of "property." But in so doing, he unwittingly proved something else as well: Ayn Rand was irrefutably correct when she made the perceptive—the seminal— identification that, from the very beginning of our country:

> America's inner contradiction was the altruist-collectivist ethics. Altruism is incompatible with freedom, with capitalism and with individual rights. One cannot combine the pursuit of happiness with the moral status of a sacrificial animal.*

These ethics formed the foundation on which slavery rested. These ethics consigned an entire race of noncitizens in America to the degrading role of sacrificial animals.

Probably more than any other case in the history of American constitutional law, *Dred Scott* reveals where the unstated premises of altruism-collectivism-statism necessarily lead the society which holds them—and the terrible consequences for those unfortunate enough to feel their weight.

It took a constitutional amendment to erase *Dred Scott* from the Supreme Court Reports. This should be cause, not for satisfaction, but for deep concern.

Enactment of the Thirteenth Amendment, though it brought the long-overdue abolition of slavery, was a mixed blessing.

To understand why, one must first understand something basic about the nature of our Constitution and its unique relationship to the Bill of Rights.

---

* Ayn Rand, "Man's Rights," *The Virtue of Selfishness* (The New American Library, 1965), p. 127.

8.

CONCLUSION

Tyranny, like hell, is not easily conquered; yet we have this consequence with us, that the harder the conflict, the more glorious the triumph.

—*Thomas Paine*

The Declaration of Independence* was a stirring appeal emanating from a previously unheard-of political philosophy, one which held that man (at least *some men*) possessed unalienable rights. It was a statement of guiding principle for a new nation. As such, it had to be translated into, and implemented by, a considerably more concrete charter of government. The Constitution of the United States of America became that charter.[†]

If one analyzes the American Constitution—omitting strictly nuts-and-bolts details like organization of the House of Representatives, the electoral college, etc.—it is at once apparent that the Founding Fathers masterfully reduced the complex machinery of a representative republic to its barest essentials. The Preamble established the

---

* See Appendix "A," where the Declaration of Independence is set forth.
† See Appendix "B," where the Constitution and all of its Amendments are set forth.

Constitution's purpose:

> We the People of the United States, in Order to form a more perfect Union, establish Justice, insure domestic Tranquility, provide for the common defence, promote the general Welfare, and secure the Blessings of Liberty to ourselves and our Posterity, do ordain and establish this Constitution for the United States of America.

To accomplish these objects, the Constitution contained a mere six Articles, delegating power from the people to their newly created federal government.* The first three Articles—legislative, executive, judicial—created separate departments to carry on the basic activities of a national government. Article IV dealt with the relationship of the federal government to its constituent states, and Article V with the machinery for amendment. Article VI established supremacy of the federal government over the states.

Although the Constitution plainly constituted only a delegation of power to the new central (federal) government (nowhere even suggesting a relinquishment of the people's unalienable rights), and although it contained many explicit and implicit "checks and balances" to federal power, fear of the new government remained widespread (as exemplified by the two Constitutional Convention delegates from New York State, Yates and Lansing, who flatly refused to sign the document). †

That fear led to a vociferous battle over the Constitution's ratification, ‡ and a major issue in the battle was the absence of a bill of rights. Most delegates simply believed that a bill of rights was unnecessary. The document they were drafting, after all, was strictly limited in nature: *only* express powers were being delegated, with the federal government possessing no other powers. How then could rights be insecure? Indeed, the Constitutional Convention debates reveal that the only time the question of a bill of rights was raised on the floor, it received short shrift.

---

* Article VII dealt, very briefly, with ratification.

† Hamilton, alone, signed for New York, making it possible for the Constitution to read: "done in Convention by the Unanimous Consent of the *States* present. . . . "; emphasis added.

‡ The whole story, though fascinating, is too lengthy and complicated to be recounted in detail here. There is, however, substantial literature on the subject.

Still, some people so deplored the absence of a bill of rights in the new Constitution that their distrust threatened ratification. The problem, it was finally recognized, had to be addressed, and, if possible, dealt with. One of the most brilliant of the Founding Fathers, certainly one of their best legal minds, tried. Against the necessity of including a bill of rights in the Constitution, Alexander Hamilton argued in *The Federalist* that:

It has been several times truly remarked that bills of rights are, in their origin, stipulations between kings and their subjects, abridgements of prerogative in favor of privilege, reservations of rights not surrendered to the prince. Such was Magna Charta, obtained by the barons, sword in hand, from King John. Such were the subsequent confirmations of that charter by succeeding princes. Such was the *Petition of Right* assented to by Charles I, in the beginning of his reign. Such, also, was the Declaration of Right presented by the Lords and Commons to the Prince of Orange in 1688, and afterwards thrown into the form of an act of parliament called the Bill of Rights. It is evident, therefore, that, according to their primitive signification, they have no application to constitutions, professedly founded upon the power of the people, and executed by their immediate representatives and servants. Here, in strictness, the people surrender nothing; and as they retain everything they have no need of particular reservations. "We, the People of the United States, to secure the blessings of liberty to ourselves and our posterity, do *ordain* and *establish* this Constitution for the United States of America." Here is a better recognition of popular rights, than volumes of those aphorisms which make the principal figure in several of our State bills of rights, and which would sound much better in a treatise of ethics than in a constitution of government.

* * *

I go further, and affirm that bills of rights, in the sense and to the extent in which they are contended for, are not only unnecessary in the proposed Constitution, but would even be dangerous. They would contain various exceptions to powers not granted; and, on this very account, would afford a colorable pretext to claim more than were granted. For why declare that things shall not be done which there is no power to do? Why, for instance, should it be said that the liberty of the press shall not be restrained, when no power is given by which restrictions may be imposed? I will not contend that such a provision would confer a regulating power; but it is evident that it would furnish, to men disposed to usurp, a plausible pretence for claiming that power.*

Putting aside how much of Hamilton's argument stemmed from conviction and how much from mere advocacy, he made two telling points.

First, bills of rights were, traditionally, restrictions on sovereign prerogative wrung by subjects out of a monarch who concededly possessed all power except that which was voluntarily relinquished. But in the United States, where there was no sovereign, no royal prerogative, no power anywhere except in the people or their delegatee, there was no need to recoup from our government, in a bill of rights, that which it had never possessed.

Second, since the federal government had not been delegated any power to violate the rights of its citizens, a bill of rights would make "exceptions to powers not granted." More specifically, since the Constitution had delegated no power to the federal government to abridge speech, press or religion, no power to compel self-incrimination or make warrantless searches and seizures, no power to violate any of the countless other rights possessed by a free people, then to draft a bill of rights prohibiting government from expressly abridging those rights was unnecessary. And dangerous. For once a specific enumeration of certain rights *was* made, Hamilton rightly pointed out, what would be the status of other rights which, for one reason or another, were not part of the enumeration? Would they be less secure? Nonexistent? What of future literalists on our Supreme Court Bench? Would they look to a list of rights and, not finding this or that right spelled out in black and white, dismiss the right out-of-hand?

Hamilton did not exaggerate this danger. Nearly two hundred years later, for example (as we saw in *Griswold* v. *Connecticut*), Justice Black, unable to find on the list the right to use contraceptives, held the right nonexistent.

The power of Hamilton's arguments carried the day, and the new Constitution eventually was ratified—but not without strong reservations, and even stronger recommendations. Several states ratified only after George Washington, throwing his personal prestige into the

---

* *The Federalist*, No. 84 (Hamilton) (The Modern Library, Random House), pp. 558-559; emphasis in original.

fight, suggested that the desired guarantees could be added later as amendments. Some states proposed amendments—at least 125 in number. Some states expected a bill of rights to be introduced in the First Congress.

And so it was. To some, its sponsor, James Madison, co-pamphleteer with Hamilton and Jay of *The Federalist*, might have seemed the last person who would want a bill of rights. In fact, Madison seemed to harbor some reservations about it. As the Supreme Court would later observe, Madison introduced a bill of rights proposal at the First Congress, "to quiet the apprehension of many, that without some such declaration of rights, the government would assume, and might be held to possess, the power to trespass upon those rights of persons and property which by the Declaration of Independence were affirmed to be unalienable * * * ."[1]

Cognizant on the one hand of "the apprehension of many," and on the other of the cogent anti-bill of rights argument in *The Federalist*, No. 84, Madison declared:

> It has been objected also against a Bill of Rights, that, by enumerating particular exceptions to the grant of power, it would disparage those rights which were not placed in that enumeration; and it might follow, by implication, that those rights which were not singled out, were intended to be assigned into the hands of the General Government, and were consequently insecure. This is one of the most plausible arguments I have ever heard urged against the admission of a bill of rights into this system; but, I conceive, that it may be guarded against. I have attempted it. . . . *

Madison's attempt reflected his perfect grasp of the problem: how to list, and thus assure, certain rights—speech, press, religion, assembly, search and seizure, no self-incrimination, compulsory process and the rest—without making it appear that their enumeration was exhaustive? His solution was to enumerate rights and, at the same time and in the same place, *reserve* all rights not enumerated. To accomplish this crucial reservation of unenumerated rights, Madison proposed the following amendment:

---

* Gales' and Seaton's "Annals of Congress," Monday, June 8, 1789.

The exceptions here or elsewhere in the Constitution, made in favor
of particular rights, shall not be so construed as to diminish the just
importance of other rights retained by the people, or as to enlarge the
powers delegated by the Constitution; but [the inclusion of particular
rights should be understood] either as actual limitations of such powers,
or as inserted merely for greater caution.*

This proposed amendment, along with what were to become the
first eight amendments to the Constitution, went to a committee
composed of one member from each state. Within a week, the
committee had adopted the following foreshortened version of Madison's proposal: "The enumeration in the Constitution, of certain
rights, shall not be construed to deny or disparage others retained by
the people."

Not one word of this language was changed by House or Senate.
The Ninth Amendment passed with virtually no debate.

Was Hamilton right? Or was Madison? Would we have been better
off sticking to Hamilton's "delegation of power" view of the Constitution, with no specific enumeration of rights? Or have we retained
whatever measure of freedom we still possess only because of
Madison's enumeration *and* reservation of rights? When three points
are considered, the answer to a hard question becomes clear.

First, altruism and collectivism have permeated political-legal
thinking and monopolized government institutions (especially our
courts and legislatures) from the very beginning of this nation's
existence. A cogent illustration from a Supreme Court that was less
than ten years old:

It seems to me, that *the right of property*, in its origin, could only
arise from compact express, or implied, and I think it the better opinion,
that the right, as well as the mode, or manner, of acquiring property, and
of alienating or transferring, inheriting, or transmitting it, *is conferred
by society.* . . . [2]

* * *

The ideas of natural justice are regulated by no fixed standard: the
ablest and the purest men have differed upon the subject; and all that the
Court could properly say, in such an event, would be, that the

---

* Gales' and Seaton's "Annals of Congress," Monday, June 8, 1789.

Legislature (possessed of an equal right of opinion) had passed an act which, in the opinion of the judges, was inconsistent with the abstract principles of natural justice.[3]

* * *

Some of the most necessary and important acts of Legislation are, on the contrary, founded upon the principle, that *private rights must yield to public exigencies*. Highways are run through private grounds. Fortifications, light-houses, and other public edifices, are necessarily sometimes built upon the soil owned by individuals. In such, and similar cases, if the owners should refuse voluntarily to accommodate the public, *they must be constrained, as far as the public necessities* require; and justice is done, by allowing them a reasonable equivalent. Without the possession of this power the operations of Government would often be obstructed, and *society itself would be endangered.**

Second, altruism and collectivism was the motivating force behind every decision discussed in this book *despite* the heavy counterweight of such specific constitutional guaranties as the First Amendment, the Contract Clause and Due Process.

Third, whenever altruism and collectivism, with their statist consequences, have pinched too tight, whenever it was widely felt that some governmental policy or action (like slavery) had gone "too far," the American people, realizing that normal political-legal processes were inadequate or not forthcoming, invoked their ultimate weapon for change, the Constitutional amendment. This was their way of protecting themselves from an unresponsive government.

Hamilton, it turns out, was dead wrong. A bill of rights, far from being dangerous, proved to be an utter necessity. Its absence would by now probably have proved fatal to our nation. Certain amendments, among them the Thirteenth (antislavery) and Nineteenth (women's suffrage), are, on the one hand, eloquent reminders of how we have been pushed to the wall in our attempt to protect individual rights, and, on the other, sad confessions that such important rights were so insecure as to require our tinkering with the Constitution itself in order to protect them.

But this "last ditch" approach to protecting rights has two inherent, and serious problems.

---

* *Calder* v. *Bull*, 3 Dallas (U.S.) 386, 400 (1798), by Justice Iredell; emphasis added.

First, amending the Constitution so that a substantial number of people can translate their personal values into law is desirable when the goal and result is to *protect* rights (as with the Thirteenth and Nineteenth Amendments). It is undesirable when the goal and result is to *violate* rights (as with a proposed antiabortion amendment). The danger here is that by removing the fight over individual rights from legislature and court and elevating it to the more rarefied atmosphere of constitutional amendment, we may lose sight of the fact that it would be as *wrong* to violate rights through a Thirtieth or Thirty-Fifth Amendment as it would be to violate them through a Virginia sterilization law or a Supreme Court's *Dred Scott* decision. If one accepts that people have no right to subordinate the individual to society's wishes through local, state or federal laws, or judicial interpretation of those laws, why should larger numbers of those same people be deemed to have that right? Did the teetotalers, who imposed their hatred of liquor on whole cities and even states, suddenly acquire legitimacy when, as prohibitionists, they were able to force their personal values on the entire country through the Eighteenth Amendment?

Where is the logic in arch-liberal William O. Douglas's argument that it is immoral for a community school board to censor our books or the Supreme Court to decide which movies we can see, but moral for three-quarters of the states—i.e., larger numbers of self-appointed censors—to do both?

There is a second problem inherent in the constitutional amendment process: the danger of relying too much on its effectiveness. Those who would do battle for individual rights cannot afford to regard the process as their ultimate weapon, and a constitutional amendment as the ultimate victory. Amendments, even when proper, are not necessarily effective. Did the Constitution's prohibition of any law "impairing the obligation of contracts" help holders of gold clause obligations (*Gold Clause Cases*), of defaulted mortgages (*Blaisdell*), or parties to racially restrictive covenants (*Shelly* v. *Kraemer*)? Was the First Amendment's prohibition of laws affecting free exercise of religion, speech and press of use to a Mormon polygamist (*Reynolds* v. *United States*), or to purveyors of pornography (*Miller, Paris Adult Theater*)? Did the Fifth Amendment's prohibition against taking private property without just compensation assist Goldblatt in his battle with the Town of Hempstead? The "exclusion" of Japanese-

Americans was held constitutional (*Korematsu*); so was forced labor (*Butler* v. *Perry*); wage and hour legislation (*Muller, West Coast Hotel*); control of individual agricultural production for home consumption (*Wickard* v. *Filburn*); civil rights public accommodation laws (*Katzenbach, Heart of Atlanta Motel*); racial quotas (*Fullilove*); forced sterilization (*Buck* v. *Bell*); zoning (*Euclid* v. *Ambler Realty Co.*); public use of private property (*PruneYard*); Sunday "Blue Laws" (*Braunfeld*); legal tender (*Knox* v. *Lee*). Even conscription (*Selective Draft Law Cases*).

Even slavery (*Dred Scott* v. *Sanford*).

These cases, and the others discussed in this book, illustrate my two-part theme. As to the major part—that the altruist-collectivist ethics are, and always have been, at the root of America's political-legal system, and are, and always have been, implemented by statism—no further elaboration is necessary. It is in the case of the minor part of my theme—that liberals and conservatives *in principle* hold the same basic ethical values—that more can be said. These values, as we have seen, may show up explicitly, more often implicitly, but they are there for the discerning eye to see. What makes arch-conservative Justice McReynolds, for example, force a Jake Butler to labor on county roads—if not the same premise that makes arch-liberal Justice Douglas force an exclusionary order on a Toyosaburo Korematsu? What do the liberal proponents of interference in the marketplace of *commerce* have in common with the conservative proponents of interference in the marketplace of *pornography*—or, more to the point, how do they really differ?

The justices whose pronouncements I have spotlighted differ, of course, in their formal political affiliations and general political attitudes; in the pet causes they espouse at the expense of the causes they don't; in the nature and degree of their contradictions. As for the *fundamental* sameness of their ideology, however, Ayn Rand provides a brilliant explanation:

> The division between the conservative and the liberal viewpoints in the opinions of the Supreme Court, is sharper and clearer than in less solemn writings or in purely political debates. By the nature of its task, the Supreme Court has to and does become the voice of philosophy.

The necessity to deal with principles makes the members of the Supreme Court seem archetypical of the ideas—almost, of the soul—of the two political camps they represent. They were not chosen as archetypes: in the undefined, indeterminate, contradictory chaos of political views loosely labeled "conservative" and "liberal," it would be impossible to choose an essential characteristic or a typical representative. Yet, as one reads the Supreme Court's opinions, the essential premises stand out with an oddly bright, revealing clarity— and one grasps that under all the lesser differences and inconsistencies of their followers, *these* are the basic premises of one political camp or of the other. It is almost as if one were seeing not these antagonists' philosophy, but their sense of life.

* * *

The conservatives want freedom to act in the material realm; they tend to oppose government control of production, of industry, of trade, of business, of physical goods, of material wealth. But they advocate government control of man's spirit, i.e., man's consciousness; they advocate the State's right to impose censorship, to determine moral values, to create and enforce a governmental establishment of morality, to rule the intellect. The liberals want freedom to act in the spiritual realm; they oppose censorship, they oppose government control of ideas, of the arts, of the press, of education (note their concern with "academic freedom"). But they advocate governmental control of material production, of business, of employment, of wages, of profits, of all physical property—they advocate it all the way down to total expropriation.

* * *

... *each camp wants to control the realm it regards as metaphysically important* ....

... neither camp has permitted itself to observe that force is a killer in both realms.... *

If force has supplanted freedom in what came close to being this sweet land of liberty, where does America go from here?

I offer two answers.

The first is exemplified by the following political party platform, whose planks few people in this country would regard as unusual today (most of the platform having long ago been enacted into

---

* Ayn Rand, "Censorship: Local and Express," *The Ayn Rand Letter*, Vol. II, No. 25, September 10, 1973, p. 2-3; emphasis in original.

American law):

> We ask that the government undertake the obligation above all of providing citizens with adequate opportunity for employment and earning a living.
>
> The activities of the individual must not be allowed to clash with the interests of the community, but must take place within its confines and be for the good of all.
>
> We demand profit sharing in big business.
>
> We demand a broad extension of care for the aged.
>
> We demand . . . the greatest possible consideration of small business in the purchases of the national, state, and municipal governments.
>
> In order to make possible to every capable and industrious [citizen] the attainment of higher education and thus the achievement of a post of leadership, the government must provide an all-around enlargement of our education . . . we demand the education at government expense of gifted children of poor parents. . . .
>
> The government must undertake the improvement of public health— by protecting mother and child, by prohibiting child labor . . . by the greatest possible support for all clubs concerned with the physical education of youth.
>
> [W]e combat the . . . materialistic spirit within and without us, and are convinced that a permanent recovery . . . can only proceed from within on the foundation of
>
> *The Common Good Before the Individual Good.* *

The architects of this party platform knew, too well, the meaning and implications of subordinating the individual to society through government force—indeed, they constructed an entire regime on the platform.

It was adopted on February 24, 1920. In Munich. By the National Socialist Party of Germany.

By the Nazis.

But we can go in a far different direction, now that we know where our nation went wrong, now that we know the nature and extent of America's inner contradiction. We have seen how the altruist-

---

* *Der Nationalsozialismus-Dokumente* 1933-1945, edited by Walther Hofer, Fischer Buecherei, Frankfurt am Main, 1957 (pp. 29-31); emphasis in original.

collectivist ethics have consistently motivated Supreme Court decision making. We have seen, as a result, how statist power has spiraled out of control at the expense of the individual. We know now that those ethics, and their inevitable consequences, must, once and for all, be purged from our system.

As the cases examined in this book amply demonstrate, concrete opportunities abound.

We can work to eliminate government's interference with the marketplace, allowing the economic aspects of capitalism to operate freely and the law of supply and demand to supplant political fiat.

We can work to end government's confiscation of private property and its nullification of private contracts, securing to individuals what is rightly theirs.

We can work to halt government's suppression of speech, ensuring freedom of communication and the unfettered exchange of ideas.

But these efforts, and others, to get government off our backs cannot succeed until liberals and conservatives alike realize that, however one fights for freedom, the struggle must be made with ruthless consistency—whether the battleground be in the legislature, in court, in the classroom, in books and articles. There is no more time for contradictions: for liberals to oppose censorship, but endorse antitrust laws; for conservatives to oppose zoning, but endorse the draft. If we are to become truly free, liberals and conservatives must understand, once and for all, that they cannot be selective about protecting those values important to *them* while violating others they deem unimportant.

Freedom will only come to America when our intellectual leaders reject altruism-collectivism-statism and replace it with an unyielding commitment to *individual rights*. We must return to the basic principle of our Declaration of Independence: we *are* created equal; as individuals, we *do* possess unalienable rights; we *have* a right to our life and our liberty and the pursuit of our own happiness. It is *we* who created government, and it is government which derives its just powers from *our* consent.

Once we fully understand and consistently implement that principle, then, as Tom Paine observed in *Common Sense* two centuries ago: "[w]e have it in our power to begin the world over again."

APPENDICES

Appendix A

DECLARATION OF INDEPENDENCE

July 4, 1776

THE UNANIMOUS DECLARATION
OF THE
THIRTEEN UNITED STATES OF AMERICA.

WHEN, in the course of human events, it becomes necessary for one people to dissolve the political bands which have connected them with another, and to assume, among the powers of the earth, the separate and equal station to which the laws of nature and of nature's God entitle them, a decent respect to the opinions of mankind requires that they should declare the causes which impel them to the separation.

We hold these truths to be self-evident: that all men are created equal; that they are endowed, by their Creator, with certain unalienable rights; that among these are life, liberty, and the pursuit of happiness. That to secure these rights, governments are instituted among men, deriving their just powers from the consent of the governed; that whenever any form of government becomes destructive of these ends, it is the right of the people to alter or to abolish it, and to institute a new government, laying its foundation on such principles, and organizing its powers in such form, as to them shall seem most likely to effect their safety and happiness. Prudence, indeed, will dictate, that governments long established, should not be changed for light and transient causes; and accordingly all experience hath shown, that mankind are more disposed to suffer, while evils are sufferable, than to right themselves by abolishing the forms to which they are accustomed. But when a long train of abuses and usurpations, pursuing invariably the same object, evinces a design to reduce them under absolute despotism, it is their right, it is their duty, to throw off such government, and to provide new guards for their future security. Such has been the patient sufferance of these colonies; and such is now the necessity which constrains them to alter their former systems of government. The history of the present King of Great Britain is a history of repeated injuries and usurpations, all having in direct object the establishment of an absolute tyranny over these states. To prove this, let facts be submitted to a candid world.

He has refused his assent to laws the most wholesome and necessary for the public good.

He has forbidden his governors to pass laws of immediate and pressing importance, unless suspended in their operation till his assent should be obtained; and when so suspended, he has utterly neglected to attend to them.

He has refused to pass other laws for the accommodation of large districts of people, unless those people would relinquish the right of representation in the legislature; a right inestimable to them, and formidable to tyrants only. He has called together legislative bodies at places unusual, uncomfortable, and distant from the depository of their public records, for the sole purpose of fatiguing them into compliance with his measures.

He has dissolved representative houses repeatedly, for opposing, with manly firmness, his invasions on the rights of the people.

He has refused for a long time, after such dissolutions, to cause others to be elected; whereby the legislative powers, incapable of annihilation, have returned to the people at large for their exercise; the state remaining, in the mean time, exposed to all the dangers of invasions from without, and convulsions within.

He has endeavored to prevent the population of these States; for that purpose obstructing the laws for naturalization of foreigners; refusing to pass others to encourage their migrations hither, and raising the conditions of new appropriations of lands.

He has obstructed the administration of justice, by refusing his assent to laws for establishing judiciary powers.

He has made judges dependent on his will alone, for the tenure of their offices, and the amount and payment of their salaries.

He has erected a multitude of new offices, and sent hither swarms of officers, to harass our people, and eat out their substance.

He has kept among us, in times of peace, standing armies, without the consent of our legislatures.

He has affected to render the military independent of, and superior to the civil power.

He has combined with others to subject us to a jurisdiction foreign to our constitution, and unacknowledged by our laws; giving his assent to their acts of pretended legislation:

For quartering large bodies of armed troops among us;

For protecting them, by a mock trial, from punishment for any murders which they should commit on the inhabitants of these States;

For cutting off our trade with all parts of the world;

For imposing taxes on us without our consent;

For depriving us, in many cases, of the benefits of trial by jury;

For transporting us beyond seas to be tried for pretended offences;

For abolishing the free system of English laws in a neighbouring province, establishing therein an arbitrary government, and enlarging its boundaries, so as to render it at once an example and fit instrument for introducing the same absolute rule into these colonies;

For taking away our charters, abolishing our most valuable laws, and altering fundamentally the forms of our governments;

For suspending our own legislatures, and declaring themselves invested with power to legislate for us in all cases whatsoever.

He has abdicated government here, by declaring us out of his protection, and waging war against us.

He has plundered our seas, ravaged our coasts, burnt our towns, and destroyed the lives of our people.

He is at this time transporting large armies of foreign mercenaries to complete the works of death, desolation, and tyranny, already begun with circumstances of cruelty and perfidy, scarcely paralleled in the most barbarous ages, and totally unworthy the head of a civilized nation.

He has constrained our fellow-citizens, taken captive on the high seas, to bear arms against their country, to become the executioners of their friends and brethren, or to fall themselves by their hands.

He has excited domestic insurrections amongst us, and has endeavoured to bring on the inhabitants of our frontiers the merciless Indian savages, whose known rule of warfare is an undistinguished destruction of all ages, sexes, and conditions.

In every stage of these oppressions we have petitioned for redress in the most humble terms. Our repeated petitions have been answered only by repeated injury. A prince, whose character is thus marked by every act which may define a tyrant, is unfit to be the ruler of a free people.

Nor have we been wanting in attentions to our British brethren. We have warned them, from time to time, of attempts by their legislature to extend an unwarrantable jurisdiction over us. We have reminded them of the circumstances of our emigration and settlement here. We have appealed to their native justice and magnanimity, and we have conjured them by the ties of our common kindred to disavow these usurpations, which would inevitably interrupt our connexions and correspondence. They too have been deaf to the voice of justice and of consanguinity. We must, therefore, acquiesce in the necessity which denounces our separation, and hold them, as we hold the rest of mankind, enemies in war, in peace friends.

We, therefore, the representatives of the UNITED STATES OF AMERICA, in General Congress assembled, appealing to the Supreme Judge of the world for the rectitude of our intentions, do, in the name, and by authority of the good people of these colonies, solemnly publish and declare, That these United Colonies are, and of right ought to be, FREE and INDEPENDENT STATES; that they are absolved from all allegiance, to the British crown, and that all political connexion between them and the state of Great Britain is, and ought to be, totally dissolved; and that, as FREE and INDEPENDENT STATES, they have full power to levy war, conclude peace, contract alliances, establish commerce, and to do all other acts and things which INDEPENDENT STATES may of right do. And for the support of this Declaration, with a firm reliance on the protection of DIVINE PROVIDENCE, we mutually pledge to each other our lives, our fortunes, and our sacred honour.

Appendix B

THE CONSTITUTION
OF THE
UNITED STATES OF AMERICA

We the People of the United States, in Order to form a more perfect Union, establish Justice, insure domestic Tranquility, provide for the common defence, promote the general Welfare, and secure the Blessings of Liberty to ourselves and our Posterity, do ordain and establish this Constitution for the United States of America.

ARTICLE I.

SECTION 1. All legislative Powers herein granted shall be vested in a Congress of the United States, which shall consist of a Senate and a House of Representatives.

SECTION 2. The House of Representatives shall be composed of Members chosen every second Year by the People of the several States, and the Electors in each State shall have the Qualifications requisite for Electors of the most numerous Branch of the State Legislature.

No person shall be a Representative who shall not have attained to the Age of twenty five Years, and been seven Years a Citizen of the United States, and who shall not, when elected, be an Inhabitant of the State in which he shall be chosen.

Representatives and direct Taxes shall be apportioned among the several States which may be included within this Union, according to their respective Numbers, which shall be determined by adding to the whole Number of free Persons, including those bound to Service for a Term of Years, and excluding Indians not taxed, three fifths of all other Persons. The actual Enumeration shall be made within three Years after the first Meeting of the Congress of the United States, and within every subsequent Term of ten Years, in such Manner as they shall by Law direct. The Number of Representatives shall not exceed one for every thirty Thousand, but each State shall have at Least one Representative; and until such enumeration shall be made, the State of New Hampshire shall be entitled to chuse three, Massachusetts eight, Rhode Island and Providence Plantations one, Connecticut five, New-York six, New Jersey four, Pennsylvania eight, Delaware one, Maryland six, Virginia ten, North Carolina five, South Carolina five, and Georgia three.

When vacancies happen in the Representation from any State, the Executive Authority thereof shall issue Writs of Election to fill such Vacancies.

The House of Representatives shall chuse their Speaker and other Officers; and shall have the sole Power of Impeachment.

SECTION 3. The Senate of the United States shall be composed of two Senators from each State, chosen by the Legislature thereof, for six Years; and each Senator shall have one vote.

Immediately after they shall be assembled in Consequence of the first Election, they shall be divided as equally as may be into three Classes. The Seats of the Senators of the first Class shall be vacated at the Expiration of the second Year, of the second Class at the Expiration of the fourth Year, and of the third Class at the Expiration of the sixth Year, so that one third may be chosen every second Year; and if Vacancies happen by Resignation, or otherwise, during the Recess of the Legislature of any State, the Executive thereof may make temporary Appointments until the next Meeting of the Legislature, which shall then fill such Vacancies.

No Person shall be a Senator who shall not have attained to the Age of thirty Years, and been nine Years a Citizen of the United States, and who shall not, when elected, be an Inhabitant of that State for which he shall be chosen.

The Vice President of the United States shall be President of the Senate, but shall have no Vote, unless they be equally divided.

The Senate shall chuse their other Officers, and also a President pro tempore, in the Absence of the Vice President, or when he shall exercise the Office of President of the United States.

The Senate shall have the sole Power to try all Impeachments. When sitting for that Purpose, they shall be on Oath or Affirmation. When the President of the United States is tried the Chief Justice shall preside: And no Person shall be convicted without the Concurrence of two thirds of the Members present.

Judgment in Cases of Impeachment shall not extend further than to removal from Office, and disqualification to hold and enjoy any Office of honor, Trust or Profit under the United States: but the Party convicted shall nevertheless be liable and subject to Indictment, Trial, Judgment and Punishment, according to Law.

SECTION 4. The Times, Places and Manner of holding Elections for Senators and Representatives, shall be prescribed in each State by the Legislature thereof; but the Congress may at any time by Law make or alter such Regulations, except as to the Places of chusing Senators.

The Congress shall assemble at least once in every Year, and such Meeting shall be on the first Monday in December, unless they shall by Law appoint a different Day.

SECTION 5. Each House shall be the Judge of the Elections, Returns and Qualifications of its own Members, and a Majority of each shall constitute a Quorum to do Business; but a smaller Number may adjourn from day to day, and may be authorized to compel the Attendance of absent Members, in such Manner, and under such Penalties as each House may provide.

Each House may determine the Rules of its Proceedings, punish its Members for disorderly Behaviour, and, with the Concurrence of two thirds, expel a Member.

Each House shall keep a Journal of its Proceedings, and from time to time publish the same, excepting such Parts as may in their Judgment require Secrecy; and the Yeas and Nays of the Members of either House on any questions shall, at the Desire of one fifth of those Present, be entered on the Journal.

Neither House, during the Session of Congress, shall, without the Consent of the other, adjourn for more than three days, nor to any other Place than that in which the two Houses shall be sitting.

SECTION 6. The Senators and Representatives shall receive a Compensation for their Services, to be ascertained by Law, and paid out of the Treasury of the United States. They shall in all Cases, except Treason, Felony and Breach of the Peace, be privileged from Arrest during their Attendance at the Session of their respective Houses, and in going to and returning from the same; and for any Speech or Debate in either House, they shall not be questioned in any other Place.

No Senator or Representative shall, during the Time for which he was elected, be appointed to any civil Office under the Authority of the United States, which shall have been created, or the Emoluments whereof shall have been encreased during such time; and no Person holding any Office under the United States, shall be a Member of either House during his Continuance in Office.

SECTION 7. All Bills for raising Revenue shall originate in the House of Representatives; but the Senate may propose or concur with amendments as on other Bills.

Every Bill which shall have passed the House of Representatives and the Senate, shall, before it become a Law, be presented to the President of the United States; If he approve he shall sign it, but if not he shall return it, with his Objections to that House in which it shall have originated, who shall enter the Objections at large on their Journal, and proceed to reconsider it. If after such Reconsideration two thirds of that House shall agree to pass the Bill, it shall be sent, together with the Objections, to the other House, by which it shall likewise be reconsidered, and if approved by two thirds of that House, it shall become a Law. But in all such Cases the Votes of both Houses shall be determined by Yeas and Nays, and the Names of the Persons voting for and against the Bill shall be entered on the Journal of each House respectively. If any Bill shall not be returned by the President within ten Days (Sunday excepted) after it shall have been presented to him, the Same shall be a Law, in like Manner as if he had signed it, unless the Congress by their Adjournment prevent its Return, in which Case it shall not be a law.

Every Order, Resolution, or Vote to which the Concurrence of the Senate and House of Represenatives may be necessary (except on a question of Adjournment) shall be presented to the President of the United States; and before the Same shall take Effect, shall be approved by him, or being disapproved by him, shall be repassed by two thirds of the Senate and House of Representatives, according to the Rules and Limitations prescribed in the Case of a Bill.

SECTION 8.   The Congress shall have Power To lay and collect Taxes, Duties, Imposts and Excises, to pay the Debts and provide for the common Defence and general Welfare of the United States; but all Duties, Imposts and Excises shall be uniform throughout the United States;

To borrow Money on the credit of the United States;

To regulate Commerce with foreign Nations, and among the several States, and with the Indian Tribes;

To establish an uniform Rule of Naturalization, and uniform Laws on the subject of Bankruptcies throughout the United States;

To coin Money, regulate the Value thereof, and of foreign Coin, and fix the Standard of Weights and Measures;

To provide for the Punishment of counterfeiting the Securities and current Coin of the United States;

To establish Post Offices and post Roads;

To promote the Progress of Science and useful Arts, by securing for limited Times to Authors and Inventors the exclusive Right to their respective Writings and Discoveries;

To constitute Tribunals inferior to the Supreme Court;

To define and punish Piracies and Felonies committed on the high Seas, and Offences against the Law of Nations;

To declare War, grant Letters of Marque and Reprisal, and make Rules concerning Captures on Land and Water;

To raise and support Armies, but no appropriation of Money to that Use shall be for a longer Term than two Years;

To provide and maintain a Navy;

To make Rules for the Government and Regulation of the land and naval Forces;

To provide for calling forth the Militia to execute the Laws of the Union, suppress Insurrections and repel Invasions;

To provide for organizing, arming, and disciplining, the Militia, and for governing such Part of them as may be employed in the Service of the United States, reserving to the States respectively, the Appointment of the Officers, and the Authority of training the Militia according to the discipline prescribed by Congress;

To exercise exclusive Legislation in all Cases whatsoever, over such District (not exceeding ten Miles square) as may, by Cession of particular States, and the Acceptance of Congress, become the Seat of the Government of the United States, and to exercise like Authority over all Places purchased by the Consent of the Legislature of the State in which the Same shall be, for the Erection of Forts, Magazines, Arsenals, dock-Yards, and other needful Buildings;—And

To make all Laws which shall be necessary and proper for carrying into Execution the foregoing Powers, and all other Powers vested by this Constitution in the Government of the United States, or in any Department or Officer thereof.

SECTION 9. The Migration or Importation of such Persons

as any of the States now existing shall think proper to admit, shall not be prohibited by the Congress prior to the Year one thousand eight hundred and eight, but a Tax or duty may be imposed on such Importation, not exceeding ten dollars for each Person.

The Privilege of the Writ of Habeas Corpus shall not be suspended, unless when in Cases of Rebellion or Invasion the public Safety may require it.

No Bill of Attainder or ex post facto Law shall be passed.

No Capitation, or other direct, Tax shall be laid, unless in Proportion to the Census of Enumeration herein before directed to be taken.

No Tax or Duty shall be laid on Articles exported from any State.

No Preference shall be given by any Regulation of Commerce or Revenue to the Ports of one State over those of another; nor shall Vessels bound to, or from, one State, be obliged to enter, clear or pay Duties in another.

No Money shall be drawn from the Treasury, but in Consequence of Appropriations made by Law; and a regular Statement and Account of the Receipts and Expenditures of all public Money shall be published from time to time.

No Title of Nobility shall be granted by the United States: And no Person holding any Office of Profit or Trust under them, shall, without the Consent of the Congress, accept of any present, Emolument, Office, or Title, of any kind whatever, from any King, Prince or foreign State.

SECTION 10. No State shall enter into any Treaty, Alliance, or Confederation; grant Letters of Marque and Reprisal; coin Money, emit Bills of Credit; make any Thing but gold and silver Coin a Tender in Payment of Debts, pass any Bill of Attainder, ex post facto Law, or Law impairing the Obligation of Contracts, or grant any Title of Nobility.

No State shall, without the Consent of the Congress, lay any Imposts or Duties on Imports or Exports, except what may be absolutely necessary for executing its inspection Laws: and the net Produce of all Duties and Imposts, laid by any State on Imports or Exports, shall be for the Use of the Treasury of the United States; and all such Laws shall be subject to the Revision and Controul of the Congress.

No State shall, without the Consent of Congress, lay any Duty of Tonnage, keep Troops, or Ships of War in time of Peace, enter into any Agreement or Compact with another State, or with a foreign Power, or engage in War, unless actually invaded, or in such imminent Danger as will not admit of delay.

ARTICLE II.

SECTION 1. The executive Power shall be vested in a President of the United States of America. He shall hold his Office during the Term of four Years, and, together with the Vice President, chosen for the same Term, be elected, as follows

Each State shall appoint, in such Manner as the Legislature thereof may direct, a Number of Electors, equal to the whole Number of Senators and Representatives to which the State may be entitled in the Congress: but no Senator or Representative, or Person holding an Office of Trust or Profit under the United States, shall be appointed an Elector.

The Electors shall meet in their respective States, and vote by Ballot for two Persons, of whom one at least shall not be an Inhabitant of the same State with themselves. And they shall make a List of all the Persons voted for, and of the Number of Votes for each; which List they shall sign and certify, and transmit sealed to the Seat of the Government of the United States, directed to the President of the Senate. The President of the Senate shall, in the Presence of the Senate and House of Representatives, open all the Certificates, and the Votes shall then be counted. The Person having the greatest Number of Votes shall be the President, if such Number be a Majority of the whole Number of Electors appointed; and if there be more than one who have such Majority, and have an equal Number of Votes, then the House of Representatives shall immediately chuse by Ballot one of them for President; and if no Person have a Majority, then from the five highest on the List the said House shall in like Manner chuse the President. But in chusing the President, the Votes shall be taken by States, the Representation from each State having one Vote; a quorum for this Purpose shall consist of a Member or Members from two thirds of the States, and a Majority of all the States shall be necessary to a Choice. In every Case, after the Choice of the President, the Person having the greatest Number of Votes of the Electors shall be the Vice President. But if there should remain two or more who have equal Votes, the Senate shall chuse from them by Ballot the Vice President.

The Congress may determine the time of chusing the Electors, and the Day on which they shall give their Votes; which Day shall be the same throughout the United States.

No Person except a natural born Citizen, or a Citizen of the United States, at the time of the Adoption of this Constitution, shall be eligible to the Office of President; neither shall any person be eligible to that Office who shall not have attained to the Age of thirty five Years, and been fourteen Years a Resident within the United States.

In Case of the Removal of the President from Office, or of his Death, Resignation, or Inability to discharge the Powers and Duties of the said Office, the Same shall devolve on the Vice President, and the Congress may by Law provide for the Case of Removal, Death, Resignation or Inability, both of the President and Vice President, declaring what Officer shall then act as President, and such Officer shall act accordingly, until the Disability be removed, or a President shall be elected.

The President shall, at stated Times, receive for his Services, a Compensation, which shall neither be encreased nor diminished during the Period for which he shall have been elected, and he shall not receive within that Period any other Emolument from the United States, or any of them.

Before he enter on the Execution of his Office, he shall take the following Oath or Affirmation:—"I do solemnly swear (or affirm) that I will faithfully execute the Office of President of the United States, and will to the best of my Ability, preserve, protect and defend the Constitution of the United States."

SECTION 2.   The President shall be Commander in Chief of the Army and Navy of the United States, and of the Militia of the several States, when called into the actual Service of the United States; he may require the Opinion, in writing, of the principal Officer in each of the executive Departments, upon any Subject relating to the Duties of their respective Offices, and he shall have Power to grant Reprieves and Pardons for Offences against the United States, except in Cases of Impeachment.

He shall have Power, by and with the Advice and Consent of the Senate, to make Treaties, provided two thirds of the Senators present concur; and he shall nominate, and by and with the Advice and Consent of the Senate, shall appoint Ambassadors, other public Ministers and Consuls, Judges of the supreme Court, and all other Officers of the United States, whose Appointments are not herein otherwise provided for, and which shall be established by Law: but the Congress may by Law vest the Appointment of such inferior Officers, as they think proper, in the President alone, in the Courts of Law, or in the Heads of Departments.

The President shall have Power to fill up all Vacancies that may happen during the Recess of the Senate, by granting Commissions which shall expire at the End of their next Session.

SECTION 3.   He shall from time to time give to the Congress Information of the State of the Union, and recommend to their Consideration such Measures as he shall judge necessary and expedient; he may, on extraordinary Occasions, convene both Houses, or either of them, and in Case of Disagreement between them, with Respect to the Time of Adjournment, he may adjourn them to such Time as he shall think proper; he shall receive Ambassadors and other public Ministers; he shall take Care that the Laws be faithfully executed, and shall Commission all the Officers of the United States.

SECTION 4.   The President, Vice President and all Civil Officers of the United States, shall be removed from Office on Impeachment for, and Conviction of, Treason, Bribery, or other high Crimes and Misdemeanors.

ARTICLE III.

SECTION 1. The judicial Power of the United States, shall be vested in one supreme Court, and in such inferior Courts as the Congress may from time to time ordain and establish. The Judges, both of the supreme and inferior Courts, shall hold their Offices during good Behaviour, and shall, at stated Times, receive for their Services, a Compensation, which shall not be diminished during their Continuance in Office.

SECTION 2. The judicial Power shall extend to all Cases, in Law and Equity, arising under this Constitution, the Laws of the United States, and Treaties made, or which shall be made, under their Authority;—to all Cases affecting Ambassadors, other public Ministers and Consuls;—to all Cases of admiralty and maritime Jurisdiction;—to Controversies to which the United States shall be a Party;—to Controversies between two or more States;—between a State and Citizens of another State;—between Citizens of different States;— between Citizens of the same State claiming Lands under Grants of different States, and between a State, or the Citizens thereof, and foreign States, Citizens or Subjects.

In all Cases affecting Ambassadors, other public Ministers and Consuls, and those in which a State shall be Party, the supreme Court shall have original jurisdiction. In all the other Cases before mentioned, the supreme Court shall have appellate Jurisdiction, both as to Law and Fact, with such Exceptions, and under such Regulations as the Congress shall make.

The Trial of all Crimes, except in Cases of Impeachment, shall be by Jury; and such Trial shall be held in the State where the said Crimes shall have been committed; but when not committed within any State, the Trial shall be at such Place or Places as the Congress may by Law have directed.

SECTION 3. Treason against the United States, shall consist only in levying War against them, or in adhering to their Enemies, giving them Aid and Comfort. No Person shall be convicted of Treason unless on the Testimony of two Witnesses to the same overt Act, or on Confession in open Court.

The Congress shall have Power to declare the Punishment of Treason, but no Attainder of Treason shall work Corruption of Blood, or Forfeiture except during the Life of the Person attainted.

ARTICLE IV.

SECTION 1. Full Faith and Credit shall be given in each State to the public Acts, Records, and judicial Proceedings of every other State. And the Congress may by general Laws prescribe the Manner in which such Acts, Records and Proceedings shall be proved, and the Effect thereof.

SECTION 2. The Citizens of each State shall be entitled to all Privileges and Immunities of Citizens in the several States.

A Person charged in any State with Treason, Felony, or other Crime, who shall flee from Justice, and be found in another State, shall on Demand of the executive Authority of the State from which he fled, be delivered up, to be removed the the State having Jurisdiction of the Crime.

No Person held to Service or Labour in one State, under the Laws thereof, escaping into another, shall, in Consequence of any Law or Regulation therein, be discharged from such Service or Labour, but shall be delivered up on Claim of the Party to whom such Service or Labour may be due.

SECTION 3. New States may be admitted by the Congress into this Union; but no new State shall be formed or erected within the Jurisdiction of any other State; nor any State be formed by the Junction of two or more States, or Parts of States, without the Consent of the Legislatures of the States concerned as well as of the Congress.

The Congress shall have Power to dispose of and make all needful Rules and Regulations respecting the Territory or other Property belonging to the United States; and nothing in this Constitution shall be so construed as to Prejudice any Claims of the United States, or of any particular State.

SECTION 4. The United States shall guarantee to every State in this Union a Republican Form of Government, and shall protect each of them against Invasion; and on Application of the Legislature, or of the Executive (when the Legislature cannot be convened) against domestic Violence.

ARTICLE V.

The Congress, whenever two thirds of both Houses shall deem it necessary, shall propose Amendments to this Constitution, or, on the Application of the Legislatures of two thirds of the several States, shall call a Convention for proposing Amendments, which, in either Case, shall be valid to all Intents and Purposes, as Part of this Constitution, when ratified by the Legislatures of three fourths of the several States, or by Conventions in three fourths thereof, as the one or the other Mode of Ratification may be proposed by the Congress; Provided that no Amendment which may be made prior to the Year One thousand eight hundred and eight shall in any Manner affect the first and fourth Clauses in the Ninth Section of the first Article; and that no State, without its Consent, shall be deprived of its equal Suffrage in the Senate.

ARTICLE VI.

All Debts contracted and Engagements entered into, before the Adoption of this Constitution, shall be as valid against the United States under this Constitution, as under the Confederation.

This Constitution, and the Laws of the United States which shall be made in Pursuance thereof; and all Treaties made, or which shall be made, under the Authority of the United States, shall be the supreme Law of the Land; and the Judges in every State shall be bound thereby, any Thing in the Constitution or Laws of any State to the Contrary notwithstanding.

The Senators and Representatives before mentioned, and the Members of the several State Legislatures, and all executive and judicial Officers, both of the United States and of the several States, shall be bound by Oath or Affirmation, to support this Constitution; but no religious Test shall ever be required as a Qualification to any Office or public Trust under the United States.

ARTICLE VII.

The Ratification of the Conventions of nine States, shall be sufficient for the Establishment of this Constitution between the States so ratifying the Same.

* * *

ARTICLES IN ADDITION TO, AND AMENDMENT OF, THE CONSTITUTION OF THE UNITED STATES OF AMERICA, PROPOSED BY CONGRESS, AND RATIFIED BY THE SEVERAL STATES, PURSUANT TO THE FIFTH ARTICLE OF THE ORIGINAL CONSTITUTION.

AMENDMENT I [1791].

Congress shall make no law respecting an establishment of religion, or prohibiting the free exercise thereof; or abridging the freedom of speech, or of the press; or the right of the people peaceably to assemble, and to petition the Government for a redress of grievances.

AMENDMENT II [1791].

A well regulated Militia, being necessary to the security of a free State, the right of the people to keep and bear Arms, shall not be infringed.

AMENDMENT III [1791].

No Soldier shall, in time of peace be quartered in any house, without the consent of the Owner, nor in time of war, but in a manner to be prescribed by law.

AMENDMENT IV [1791].

The right of the people to be secure in their persons, houses, papers, and effects, against unreasonable searches and seizures, shall not be violated, and no Warrants shall issue, but upon probable cause, supported by Oath or affirmation, and particularly describing the place to be searched, and the persons or things to be seized.

AMENDMENT V [1791].

No person shall be held to answer for a capital, or otherwise infamous crime, unless on a presentment or indictment of a Grand Jury, except in cases arising in the land or naval forces, or in the Militia, when in actual service in time of War or public danger; nor shall any person be subject for the same offence to be twice put in jeopardy of life or limb; nor shall be compelled in any criminal case to be a witness against himself, nor be deprived of life, liberty, or property, without due process of law; nor shall private property be taken for public use, without just compensation.

AMENDMENT VI [1791].

In all criminal prosecutions, the accused shall enjoy the right to a speedy and public trial, by an impartial jury of the State and district wherein the crime shall have been committed, which district shall have been previously ascertained by law, and to be informed of the nature and cause of the accusation; to be confronted with the witnesses against him; to have compulsory process for obtaining Witnesses in his favor, and to have the Assistance of Counsel for his defence.

AMENDMENT VII [1791].

In Suits at common law, where the value in controversy shall exceed twenty dollars, the right of trial by jury shall be preserved, and no fact tried by a jury, shall be otherwise re-examined in any Court of the United States, than according to the rules of the common law.

AMENDMENT VIII [1791].

Excessive bail shall not be required, nor excessive fines imposed, nor cruel and unusual punishments inflicted.

AMENDMENT IX [1791].

The enumeration in the Constitution, of certain rights, shall not be construed to deny or disparage others retained by the people.

AMENDMENT X [1791].

The powers not delegated to the United States by the Constitution, nor prohibited by it to the States, are reserved to the States respectively, or to the people.

AMENDMENT XI [1798].

The Judicial power of the United States shall not be construed to extend to any suit in law or equity, commenced or prosecuted against one of the United States by Citizens of another State, or by Citizens or Subjects of any Foreign State.

AMENDMENT XII [1804].

The Electors shall meet in their respective states and vote by ballot for President and Vice-President, one of whom, at least, shall not be an inhabitant of the same state with themselves; they shall name in their ballots the person voted for as President, and in distinct ballots the person voted for as Vice-President, and they shall make distinct lists of all persons voted for as President, and of all persons voted for as Vice-President, and of the number of votes for each, which lists they shall sign and certify, and transmit sealed to the seat of the government of the United States, directed to the President of the Senate;—The President of the Senate shall, in the presence of the Senate and House of Representatives, open all the certificates and the votes shall then be counted;—The person having the greatest number of votes for President, shall be the President, if such number be a majority of the whole number of Electors appointed; and if no person have such majority, then from the persons having the highest numbers not exceeding three on the list of those voted for as President, the House of Representatives shall choose immediately, by ballot, the President. But in choosing the President, the votes shall be taken by states, the representation from each state having one vote; a quorum for this purpose shall consist of a member or members from two-thirds of the states, and a majority of all the states shall be necessary to a choice. And if the House of Representatives shall not choose a President whenever the right of choice shall devolve upon them, before the fourth day of March next following, then the Vice-President shall act as President, as in the case of the death or other constitutional disability of the President—The person having the greatest number of votes as Vice-President, shall be the Vice-President, if such number be a majority of the whole number of Electors appointed, and if no person have a majority, then from the two highest numbers on the list, the Senate shall choose the Vice-President; a quorum for the purpose shall consist of two-thirds of the whole number of Senators, and a majority of the whole number shall be necessary to a choice. But no person constitutionally ineligible to the office of President shall be eligible to that of Vice-President of the United States.

AMENDMENT XIII [1865].

SECTION 1. Neither slavery nor involuntary servitude, except as a punishment for crime whereof the party shall have been duly convicted, shall exist within the United States, or any place subject to their jurisdiction.

SECTION 2. Congress shall have power to enforce this article by appropriate legislation.

AMENDMENT XIV [1868].

SECTION 1. All persons born or naturalized in the United States and subject to the jurisdiction thereof, are citizens of the United States and of the State wherein they reside. No State shall make or enforce any law which shall abridge the privileges or immunities of citizens of the United States; nor shall any State deprive any person of life, liberty, or property, without due process of law; nor deny to any person within its jurisdiction the equal protection of the laws.

SECTION 2. Representatives shall be apportioned among the several States according to their respective numbers, counting the whole number of persons in each State, excluding Indians not taxed. But when the right to vote at any election for the choice of electors for President and Vice President of the United States, Representatives in Congress, the Executive and Judicial officers of a State, or the members of the Legislature thereof, is denied to any of the male inhabitants of such State, being twenty-one years of age, and citizens of the United States, or in any way abridged, except for participation in rebellion, or other crime, the basis of representation therein shall be reduced in the proportion which the number of such male citizens shall bear to the whole number of male citizens twenty-one years of age in such State.

SECTION 3. No person shall be a Senator or Representative in Congress, or elector of President and Vice President, or hold any office, civil or military, under the United States, or under any State, who, having previously taken an oath, as a member of Congress, or as an officer of the United States, or as a member of any State legislature, or as an executive or judicial officer of any State, to support the Constitution of the United States, shall have engaged in insurrection or rebellion against the same, or given aid or comfort to the enemies thereof. But Congress may by a vote of two-thirds of each House, remove such disability.

SECTION 4. The validity of the public debt of the United States, authorized by law, including debts incurred for payment of pensions and bounties for services in suppressing insurrection or rebellion, shall not be questioned. But neither the United States nor any State shall assume or pay any debt or obligation incurred in aid of insurrection or rebellion against the United States, or any claim for the loss or emancipation of any slave; but all such debts, obligations and claims shall be held illegal and void.

SECTION 5. The Congress shall have power to enforce, by appropriate legislation, the provisions of this article.

AMENDMENT XV [1870].

SECTION 1. The right of citizens of the United States to

vote shall not be denied or abridged by the United States or by any State on account of race, color, or previous condition of servitude.

SECTION 2. The Congress shall have power to enforce this article by appropriate legislation.

AMENDMENT XVI [1913].

The Congress shall have power to lay and collect taxes on incomes, from whatever source derived, without apportionment among the several States, and without regard to any census or enumeration.

AMENDMENT XVII [1913].

The Senate of the United States shall be composed of two Senators from each State, elected by the people thereof, for six years; and each Senator shall have one vote. The electors in each State shall have the qualifications requisite for electors of the most numerous branch of the State legislatures.

When vacancies happen in the representation of any State in the Senate, the executive authority of such State shall issue writs of election to fill such vacancies: *Provided*, That the legislature of any State may empower the executive thereof to make temporary appointments until the people fill the vacancies by election as the legislature may direct.

This amendment shall not be so construed as to affect the election or term of any Senator chosen before it becomes valid as part of the Constitution.

AMENDMENT XVIII [1919].

SECTION 1. After one year from the ratification of this article the manufacture, sale, or transportation of intoxicating liquors within, the importation thereof into, or the exportation thereof from the United States and all territory subject to the jurisdiction thereof for beverage purposes is hereby prohibited.

SECTION 2. The Congress and the several States shall have concurrent power to enforce this article by appropriate legislation.

SECTION 3. This article shall be inoperative unless it shall have been ratified as an amendment to the Constitution by the legislatures of the several States, as provided in the Constitution, within seven years from the date of the submission hereof to the States by the Congress.

AMENDMENT XIX [1920].

The right of citizens of the United States to vote shall not be denied or abridged by the United States or by any State on account of sex.

Congress shall have power to enforce this article by appropriate legislation.

AMENDMENT XX [1933].

SECTION 1. The terms of the President and Vice President shall end at noon on the 20th day of January, and the terms of Senators and Representatives at noon on the 3d day of January, of the years in which such terms would have ended if this article had not been ratified; and the terms of their successors shall then begin.

SECTION 2. The Congress shall assemble at least once in every year, and such meeting shall begin at noon on the 3d day of January, unless they shall by law appoint a different day.

SECTION 3. If, at the time fixed for the beginning of the term of the President, the President elect shall have died, the Vice President elect shall become President. If a President shall not have been chosen before the time fixed for the beginning of his term, or if the President elect shall have failed to qualify, then the Vice President elect shall act as President until a President shall have qualified; and the Congress may by law provide for the case wherein neither a President elect nor a Vice President elect shall have qualified, declaring who shall then act as President, or the manner in which one who is to act shall be selected, and such person shall act accordingly until a President or Vice President shall have qualified.

SECTION 4. The Congress may by law provide for the case of the death of any of the persons from whom the House of Representatives may choose a President whenever the right of choice shall have devolved upon them, and for the case of the death of any of the persons from whom the Senate may choose a Vice President whenever the right of choice shall have devolved upon them.

SECTION 5. Sections 1 and 2 shall take effect on the 15th day of October following the ratification of this article.

SECTION 6. This article shall be inoperative unless it shall have been ratified as an amendment to the Constitution by the legislatures of three-fourths of the several States within seven years from the date of its submission.

AMENDMENT XXI [1933].

SECTION 1. The eighteenth article of amendment to the Constitution of the United States is hereby repealed.

SECTION 2. The transportation or importation into any State, Territory or possession of the United States for delivery or use therein of intoxicating liquors, in violation of the laws thereof, is hereby prohibited.

SECTION 3. This article shall be inoperative unless it shall have been ratified as an amendment to the Constitution by conventions in the several States, as provided in the Constitution, within seven years from the date of the submission hereof to the States by the Congress.

AMENDMENT XXII [1951].

SECTION 1. No person shall be elected to the office of the President more than twice, and no person who has held the office of President, or acted as President, for more than two years of a term to which some other person was elected President shall be elected to the office of the President more than once. But this Article shall not apply to any person holding the office of President when this Article was proposed by the Congress, and shall not prevent any person who may be holding the office of President, or acting as President, during the term within which this Article becomes operative from holding the office of President or acting as President during the remainder of such term.

SECTION 2. This article shall be inoperative unless it shall have been ratified as an amendment to the Constitution by the legislatures of three-fourths of the several States within seven years from the date of its submission to the States by the Congress.

AMENDMENT XXIII [1961].

SECTION 1.   The District constituting the seat of Government of the United States shall appoint in such manner as the Congress may direct:

A number of electors of President and Vice President equal to the whole number of Senators and Representatives in Congress to which the District would be entitled if it were a State, but in no event more than the least populous State; they shall be in addition to those appointed by the States, but they shall be considered, for the purposes of the election of President and Vice President, to be electors appointed by a State; and they shall meet in the District and perform such duties as provided by the twelfth article of amendment.

SECTION 2.   The Congress shall have power to enforce this article by appropriate legislation.

AMENDMENT XXIV [1964].

SECTION 1.   The right of citizens of the United States to vote in any primary or other election for President or Vice President, for electors for President or Vice President, or for Senator or Representative in Congress, shall not be denied or abridged by the United States or any State by reason of failure to pay any poll tax or other tax.

SECTION 2.   The Congress shall have power to enforce this article by appropriate legislation.

AMENDMENT XXV [1967].

SECTION 1.   In case of the removal of the President from office or of his death or resignation, the Vice President shall become President.

SECTION 2.   Whenever there is a vacancy in the office of the Vice President, the President shall nominate a Vice President who shall take office upon confirmation by a majority vote of both Houses of Congress.

SECTION 3. Whenever the President transmits to the President pro tempore of the Senate and the Speaker of the House of Representatives his written declaration that he is unable to discharge the powers and duties of his office, and until he transmits to them a written declaration to the contrary, such powers and duties shall be discharged by the Vice President as Acting President.

SECTION 4. Whenever the Vice President and a majority of either the principal officers of the executive departments or of such other body as Congress may by law provide, transmit to the President pro tempore of the Senate and the Speaker of the House of Representatives their written declaration that the President is unable to discharge the powers and duties of his office, the Vice President shall immediately assume the powers and duties of the office as Acting President.

Thereafter, when the President transmits to the President pro tempore of the Senate and the Speaker of the House of Representatives his written declaration that no inability exists, he shall resume the powers and duties of his office unless the Vice President and a majority of either the principal officers of the executive department or of such other body as Congress may by law provide, transmit within four days to the President pro tempore of the Senate and the Speaker of the House of Representatives their written declaration that the President is unable to discharge the powers and duties of his office. Thereupon Congress shall decide the issue, assembling within forty-eight hours for that purpose if not in session. If the Congress, within twenty-one days after receipt of the latter written declaration, or, if Congress is not in session, within twenty-one days after Congress is required to assemble, determines by two-thirds vote of both Houses that the President is unable to discharge the powers and duties of his office, the Vice President shall continue to discharge the same as Acting President; otherwise, the President shall resume the powers and duties of his office.

AMENDMENT XXVI [1971].

SECTION 1. The right of citizens of the United States, who are eighteen years of age or older, to vote shall not be denied or abridged by the United States or by any State on account of age.

SECTION 2. The Congress shall have power to enforce this article by appropriate legislation.

TABLE OF CASES

NOTES

Chapter 1

1. *Muller v. Oregon*, 208 U.S. 412, 416, 28 S.Ct. 324 (1908).
2. *West Coast Hotel Co. v. Parrish*, 300 U.S. 379, 57 S.Ct. 578 (1937).
3. *United States v. Darby*, 312 U.S. 100, 61 S.Ct. 451 (1941).
4. *Wickard v. Filburn*, 317 U.S. 111, 128, 63 S.Ct. 82, 90-91 (1942).
5. *Wickard v. Filburn*, 317 U.S. 111, 129, 63 S.Ct. 82, 91 (1942).
6. *Brown v. Board of Education*, 347 U.S. 483, 74 S.Ct. 686 (1954).
7. See Hearings Before the Senate Committee on Commerce on S. 1732, 88th Cong., 1st Sess., parts 1 and 2.
8. See Gerald Gunther, *Constitutional Law Cases and Materials*, 10th ed. (The Foundation Press, 1980), p. 203.
9. 78 Stat. 241-268.
10. *Heart of Atlanta Motel, Inc. v. United States*, 379 U.S. 241, 85 S.Ct. 348 (1964).
11. *Katzenbach v. McClung*, 379 U.S. 294, 85 S.Ct. 377 (1964).
12. Senate Report No. 872, 88th Cong., 2d Sess., 16.
13. *Runyon v. McCrary*, 427 U.S. 160, 96 S.Ct. 2586 (1976).
14. *Runyon v. McCrary*, 427 U.S. 160, 186, 96 S.Ct. 2586, 2602 (1976).
15. *Runyon v. McCrary*, 427 U.S. 160, 191, 96 S.Ct. 2586, 2604 (1976).
16. Pub.L. 95-28, 91 Stat. 116.
17. 103(f)(2).
18. 123 Cong. Rec. H1388-1389 (Feb. 23, 1977).
19. 123 Cong. Rec. H1440 (Feb. 24, 1977).
20. 123 Cong. Rec. H1440-1441 (Feb. 24, 1977).
21. *Fullilove v. Klutznick*, 448 U.S. 453, 516, 100 S.Ct. 2758, 2794 (1980).
22. *Fullilove v. Klutznick*, 448 U.S. 453, 522, 100 S.Ct. 2758, 2797 (1980).

Chapter 2

1. *Robins v. PruneYard Shopping Center*, 23 Cal. 3d 899, 910, 153 Cal.Rptr. 854, 860, 592 P.2d 341, 347 (1979).
2. *PruneYard Shopping Center v. Robins*, 447 U.S. 74, 81, 100 S.Ct. 2035, 2040 (1980).
3. Article I, section 2.
4. Article I, section 3.
5. *PruneYard Shopping Center v. Robins*, 447 U.S. 74, 84-85, 100 S.Ct. 2035, 2042 (1980).
6. 42 U.S.C. Section 1982.
7. 392 U.S. 409, 88 S.Ct. 2186 (1968).

8. *Jones v. Alfred H. Mayer Co.*, 392 U.S. 409, 443, 88 S.Ct. 2186, 2205 (1968).

9. *Jones v. Alfred H. Mayer Co.*, 392 U.S. 409, 473-474, 88 S.Ct. 2186, 2220 (1968).

10. *Jones v. Alfred H. Mayer Co.*, 392 U.S. 409, 478, 88 S.Ct. 2186, 2222 (1968).

11. *Jones v. Alfred H. Mayer Co.*, 392 U.S. 409, 445, 88 S.Ct. 2186, 2206 (1968).

12. Title VIII; see Pub.L. 90-284, 82 Stat. 81.

13. 272 U.S. 365, 47 S.Ct. 114 (1926).

14. *Euclid v. Ambler Realty Co.*, 272 U.S. 365, 384, 47 S.Ct. 114, 117 (1926).

15. *Euclid v. Ambler Realty Co.*, 272 U.S. 365, 389, 47 S.Ct. 114, 119 (1926).

16. *Village of Belle Terre v. Boraas*, 416 U.S. 1, 2, 94 S.Ct. 1536, 1537-1538 (1974).

17. *Village of Belle Terre v. Boraas*, 416 U.S. 1, 7, 94 S.Ct. 1536, 1540 (1974).

18. *Village of Belle Terre v. Boraas*, 416 U.S. 1, 9, 94 S.Ct. 1536, 1541 (1974).

19. 447 U.S. 255, 100 S.Ct. 2138 (1980).

20. *Agins v. City of Tiburon*, 447 U.S. 255, 261, 100 S.Ct. 2138, 2142 (1980).

21. *Agins v. City of Tiburon*, 447 U.S. 255, 261, 100 S.Ct. 2138, 2141-2142 (1980).

22. *Goldblatt v. Town of Hempstead*, 369 U.S. 590, 592, 82 S.Ct. 987, 989 (1962).

23. *Goldblatt v. Town of Hempstead*, 369 U.S. 590, 592, 82 S.Ct. 987, 989 (1962).

24. *Goldblatt v. Town of Hempstead*, 369 U.S. 590, 594, 82 S.Ct. 987, 990 (1962).

25. *Goldblatt v. Town of Hempstead*, 369 U.S. 590, 594-595, 82 S.Ct. 987, 990 (1962).

Chapter 3

1. 79 U.S. (12 Wall.) 457 (1871).

2. 79 U.S. at 549.

3. 290 U.S. 398, 54 S.Ct. 231 (1934).

4. *Home Building & Loan Ass'n v. Blaisdell*, 290 U.S. 398, 420, 54 S.Ct. 231, 233 (1934).

5. *Home Building & Loan Ass'n v. Blaisdell*, 290 U.S. 398, 422-423, 54 S.Ct. 231, 234 (1934).

6. *Home Building & Loan Ass'n v. Blaisdell*, 290 U.S. 398, 475, 54 S.Ct. 231, 253 (1934).

7. *Shelly v. Kraemer*, 334 U.S. 1, 4, 68 S.Ct. 836, 838 (1948).

8. *Shelly v. Kraemer*, 334 U.S. 1, 13, 68 S.Ct. 836, 842 (1948).

9. *Shelly v. Kraemer*, 334 U.S. 1, 19, 68 S.Ct. 836, 845 (1948).

Chapter 4

1. *Davis v. Beason*, 133 U.S. 333, 342, 10 S.Ct. 299, 300 (1890).

2. *Reynolds v. United States*, 98 U.S. 145, 153 (1878).

3. *Reynolds v. United States*, 98 U.S. 145, 161 (1878).

4. *Reynolds v. United States*, 98 U.S. 145, 162 (1878).

5. *Reynolds* v. *United States*, 98 U.S. 145, 164 (1878).

6. *Reynolds* v. *United States*, 98 U.S. 145, 164 (1878).

7. *Reynolds* v. *United States*, 98 U.S. 145, 165 (1878).

8. *McGowan* v. *Maryland*, 366 U.S. 420, 81 S.Ct. 1101 (1961); *Gallagher* v. *Crown Kosher Super Market of Massachusetts, Inc.*, 366 U.S. 617, 81 S.Ct. 1122 (1961); *Two Guys from Harrison-Allentown, Inc.* v. *McGinley*, 366 U.S. 582, 81 S.Ct. 1135 (1961); *Braunfeld* v. *Brown*, 366 U.S. 599, 81 S.Ct. 1144 (1961).

9. *McGowan* v. *Maryland*, 366 U.S. 420, 426, 81 S.Ct. 1101, 1105 (1961).

10. *McGowan* v. *Maryland*, 366 U.S. 420, 449, 81 S.Ct. 1101, 1117 (1961).

11. *Gallagher* v. *Crown Kosher Super Market of Massachusetts, Inc.*, 366 U.S. 617, 630-631, 81 S.Ct. 1122, 1129 (1961).

12. *Braunfeld* v. *Brown*, 366 U.S. 599, 605, 81 S.Ct. 1144, 1147 (1961).

13. *Braunfeld* v. *Brown*, 366 U.S. 599, 605-606, 81 S.Ct. 1144, 1147 (1961).

14. *Braunfeld* v. *Brown*, 366 U.S. 599, 607, 81 S.Ct. 1144, 1148 (1961).

15. *Braunfeld* v. *Brown*, 366 U.S. 599, 611, 81 S.Ct. 1104, 1150 (1961).

16. *Braunfeld* v. *Brown*, 366 U.S. 599, 614, 81 S.Ct. 1104, 1151 (1961).

17. *Braunfeld* v. *Brown*, 366 U.S. 599, 614, 81 S.Ct. 1104, 1151 (1961).

18. *Braunfeld* v. *Brown*, 366 U.S. 599, 614, 81 S.Ct. 1104, 1151 (1961).

19. *McGowan* v. *Maryland*, 366 U.S. 420, 578, 81 S.Ct. 1101, 1227 (1961).

20. *McGowan* v. *Maryland*, 366 U.S. 420, 578, 81 S.Ct. 1101, 1227 (1961).

21. *McGowan* v. *Maryland*, 366 U.S. 420, 573-574, 81 S.Ct. 1101, 1225 (1961).

Chapter 5

1. *Schenck* v. *United States*, 249 U.S. 47, 51, 39 S.Ct. 247, 248 (1919).

2. C. 30, Section 3, 40 Stat. 217, 219.

3. *Schenck* v. *United States*, 249 U.S. 47, 52, 39 S.Ct. 247, 249 (1919).

4. *Dennis* v. *United States*, 341 U.S. 494, 497, 71 S.Ct. 857, 861 (1951).

5. *Valentine* v. *Chrestensen*, 316 U.S. 52, 62 S.Ct. 920 (1942).

6. *Valentine* v. *Chrestensen*, 316 U.S. 52, 54, 62 S.Ct. 920, 921 (1942).

7. 319 U.S. 141, 63 S.Ct. 862 (1943).

8. *Martin* v. *Struthers*, 319 U.S. 141, 63 S.Ct. 862 (1943). See also *Breard*, below, at 341 U.S. 643 and 63 S.Ct. 933.

9. 341 U.S. 622, 71 S.Ct. 920 (1951).

10. See, e.g., *Murdock* v. *Pennsylvania*, 319 U.S. 105, 63 S.Ct. 870 (1943); *Jamison* v. *Texas*, 318 U.S. 413, 63 S.Ct. 669 (1943); *Thomas* v. *Collins*, above; *New York Times Co.* v. *Sullivan*, 376 U.S. 254, 84 S.Ct. 710 (1964); *Pittsburgh Press Co.* v. *Human Relations Comm'n*, 413 U.S. 376, 93 S.Ct. 2553 (1973).

11. See, e.g., *Dennis* v. *United States*, above.

12. See, e.g., *Village of Belle Terre* v. *Boraas*, above.

13. 358 U.S. 498, 79 S.Ct. 524 (1959).

14. *Virginia State Board of Pharmacy* v. *Virginia Citizens Consumer Council, Inc.*, 425 U.S. 748, 96 S.Ct. 1817 (1976).

15. See *Virginia State Board of Pharmacy* v. *Virginia Citizens Consumer Council, Inc.*, 425 U.S. 748, 762-763, 96 S.Ct. 1817, 1825-1826 (1976).

16. See *Virginia State Board of Pharmacy* v. *Virginia Citizens Consumer Council, Inc.*, 425 U.S. 748, 770, 96 S.Ct. 1817, 1830 (1976).

17. *Virginia State Board of Pharmacy* v. *Virginia Citizens Consumer Council, Inc.*, 425 U.S. 748, 763-764, 96 S.Ct. 1817, 1826 (1976).

18. *Chaplinsky* v. *New Hampshire*, 315 U.S. 568, 62 S.Ct. 766 (1942).

19. 354 U.S. 476, 77 S.Ct. 1304 (1957).

20. *Roth* v. *United States, Alberts* v. *California*, 354 U.S. 476, 485, 77 S.Ct. 1304, 1309 (1957).

21. *Roth* v. *United States, Alberts* v. *California*, 354 U.S. 476, 487, 77 S.Ct. 1304, 1310 (1957).

22. *Roth* v. *United States, Alberts* v. *California*, 354 U.S. 476, 484, 77 S.Ct. 1304, 1309 (1957).

23. *Miller* v. *California*, 413 U.S. 15, 37-38, 93 S.Ct. 2607, 2622 (1973).

24. 378 U.S. 184, 84 S.Ct. 1676 (1964).

25. *Jacobellis* v. *Ohio*, 378 U.S. 184, 197, 84 S.Ct. 1676, 1683 (1964).

26. *Jacobellis* v. *Ohio*, 378 U.S. 184, 197, 84 S.Ct. 1676, 1683 (1964).

27. 383 U.S. 413, 86 S.Ct. 975 (1966).

28. *Memoirs* v. *Massachusetts*, 383 U.S. 413, 418, 86 S.Ct. 975, 977 (1966).

29. *Paris Adult Theater I* v. *Slayton*, 413 U.S. 49, 80-82, 92 S.Ct. 2628, 2645-2646 (1973).

30. 386 U.S. 767, 87 S.Ct. 1414 (1967).

31. 413 U.S. 15, 93 S.Ct. 2607 (1973).

32. 413 U.S. 49, 93 S.Ct. 2628 (1973).

33. *Miller* v. *California*, 413 U.S. 15, 18, 93 S.Ct. 2607, 2611-2612 (1973).

34. *Miller* v. *California*, 413 U.S. 15, 19-20, 93 S.Ct. 2607, 2612 (1973).

35. *Miller* v. *California*, 413 U.S. 15, 22, 93 S.Ct. 2607, 2614 (1973).

36. *Miller* v. *California*, 413 U.S. 15, 22, 93 S.Ct. 2607, 2614 (footnote) (1973).

37. *Miller* v. *California*, 413 U.S. 15, 24, 93 S.Ct. 2607, 2615 (1973).

38. *Miller* v. *California*, 413 U.S. 15, 32-33, 93 S.Ct. 2607, 2619-2620 (1973).

39. *Miller* v. *California*, 413 U.S. 15, 25, 93 S.Ct. 2607, 2615 (1973).

40. *Miller* v. *California*, 413 U.S. 15, 25, 93 S.Ct. 2607, 2615 (1973).

41. *Miller* v. *California*, 413 U.S. 15, 26, 93 S.Ct. 2607, 2616 (1973).

42. *Miller* v. *California*, 413 U.S. 15, 34-35, 93 S.Ct. 2607, 2620-2621 (1973).

43. *Miller* v. *California*, 413 U.S. 15, 35-36, 93 S.Ct. 2607, 2621 (1973).

44. *Paris Adult Theater I* v. *Slayton*, 413 U.S. 49, 53, 93 S.Ct. 2607, 2632-2633 (1973).

45. *Paris Adult Theater I* v. *Slayton*, 413 U.S. 49, 53, 93 S.Ct. 2607, 2633 (1973).

46. *Paris Adult Theater I* v. *Slayton*, 413 U.S. 49, 57, 93 S.Ct. 2607, 2635 (1973).

47. *Paris Adult Theater I* v. *Slayton*, 413 U.S. 49, 67, 93 S.Ct. 2607, 2640 (1973).

48. *Paris Adult Theater I* v. *Slayton*, 413 U.S. 49, 65, 66, 93 S.Ct. 2607, 2639, 2640 (1973).

49. *Paris Adult Theater I* v. *Slayton*, 413 U.S. 49, 68, 93 S.Ct. 2607, 2637 (1973).

50. *Paris Adult Theater I* v. *Slayton*, 413 U.S. 49, 68, 93 S.Ct. 2607, 2641 (footnote) (1973).
51. *Paris Adult Theater I* v. *Slayton*, 413 U.S. 49, 69, 93 S.Ct. 2607, 2641 (1973).
52. *Paris Adult Theater I* v. *Slayton*, 413 U.S. 49, 58, 93 S.Ct. 2607, 2635 (1973).
53. *Paris Adult Theater I* v. *Slayton*, 413 U.S. 49, 62, 64, 93 S.Ct. 2607, 2637-2638, 2639 (1973).
54. *Paris Adult Theater I* v. *Slayton* 413 U.S. 49, 103, 93 S.Ct. 2607, 2657 (1973).
55. *Paris Adult Theater I* v. *Slayton*, 413 U.S. 49, 108-109, 93 S.Ct. 2607, 2660 (1973).
56. *Miller* v. *California*, 413 U.S. 15, 41, 46-47, 93 S.Ct. 2607, 2624, 2627 (1973).

Chapter 6

1. *State* v. *Rhinehart*, 424 P.2d 906, 907 (Wash., 1967).
2. *State* v. *Rhinehart*, 424 P.2d 906, 909 (Wash., 1967).
3. *State* v. *Rhinehart*, 424 P.2d 906, 909 (Wash., 1967).
4. 389 U.S. 832 (1967).
5. 425 U.S. 901, 96 S.Ct. 1489-1490 (1976).
6. *Doe* v. *Commonwealth's Attorney*, 403 F.Supp. 1199, 1200 (1975).
7. *Doe* v. *Commonwealth's Attorney*, 403 F.Supp. 1199, 1202 (1975).
8. *Doe* v. *Commonwealth's Attorney*, 403 F.Supp. 1199, 1202-1203 (1975).
9. *Doe* v. *Commonwealth's Attorney*, 403 F.Supp. 1199, 1201 (1975).
10. *Doe* v. *Commonwealth's Attorney*, 403 F.Supp. 1199, 1202 (1975).
11. 381 U.S. 479, 85 S.Ct. 1678 (1965).
12. General Statutes of Connecticut (1958 rev.) Section 53-32.
13. General Statutes of Connecticut (1958 rev.) Section 54-196.
14. *Griswold* v. *Connecticut*, 381 U.S. 479, 485, 85 S.Ct. 1678, 1682 (1965).
15. *Griswold* v. *Connecticut*, 381 U.S. 479, 500, 85 S.Ct. 1678, 1690 (1965).
16. *Poe* v. *Ullman*, 367 U.S. 497, 545, 81 S.Ct. 1752, 1778 (1961).
17. *Griswold* v. *Connecticut*, 381 U.S. 479, 505, 85 S.Ct. 1678, 1693 (1965).
18. *Roe* v. *Wade*, 410 U.S. 113, 139, 93 S.Ct. 705, 720 (1973).
19. *Roe* v. *Wade*, 410 U.S. 113, 140-141, 93 S.Ct. 705, 720-721 (1973).
20. *Roe* v. *Wade*, 410 U.S. 113, 152-153, 93 S.Ct. 705, 726 (1973).
21. *Roe* v. *Wade*, 410 U.S. 113, 169, 93 S.Ct. 705, 735 (1973).
22. *Roe* v. *Wade*, 410 U.S. 113, 154, 93 S.Ct. 705, 727 (1973).
23. *Roe* v. *Wade*, 410 U.S. 113, 162, 93 S.Ct. 705, 731 (1973).
24. *Roe* v. *Wade*, 410 U.S. 113, 215, 93 S.Ct. 705, 759 (1973).
25. *Roe* v. *Wade*, 410 U.S. 113, 158, 93 S.Ct. 705, 729 (1973).
26. *Roe* v. *Wade*, 410 U.S. 113, 162, 93 S.Ct. 705, 731 (1973).
27. *Roe* v. *Wade*, 410 U.S. 113, 159, 93 S.Ct. 705, 730 (1973).
28. *Roe* v. *Wade*, 410 U.S. 113, 164, 93 S.Ct. 705, 732 (1973).
29. *Roe* v. *Wade*, 410 U.S. 113, 164, 93 S.Ct. 705, 732 (1973).

30. *Roe* v. *Wade*, 410 U.S. 113, 164-165, 93 S.Ct. 705, 732 (1973).
31. *Maher* v. *Roe*, 432 U.S. 464, 466, 97 S.Ct. 2376, 2378 (1977).
32. *Maher* v. *Roe*, 432 U.S. 464, 473-474, 97 S.Ct. 2376, 2382 (1977).

Chapter 7

1. *Buck* v. *Bell*, 274 U.S. 200, 47 S.Ct. 584 (1927).
2. *Buck* v. *Bell*, 274 U.S. 200, 205, 47 S.Ct. 584 (1927).
3. 316 U.S. 535, 62 S.Ct. 1110 (1942).
4. *Skinner* v. *Oklahoma*, 316 U.S. 535, 546, 62 S.Ct. 1110, 1116 (1942).
5. *Skinner* v. *Oklahoma*, 316 U.S. 535, 544, 62 S.Ct. 1110, 1115 (1942).
6. *Butler* v. *Perry*, 240 U.S. 328, 330, 36 S.Ct. 258 (1916).
7. *Butler* v. *Perry*, 240 U.S. 328, 333, 36 S.Ct. 258, 259 (1916).

8. *Butler* v. *Perry*, 240 U.S. 328, 333, 36 S.Ct. 258, 260 (1916).
9. 7 Fed. Reg. 1407.
10. 7 Fed. Reg. 2320.
11. 56 Stat. 173, 18 U.S.C.A. Section 97A.
12. 7 Fed. Reg. 2601.
13. 7 Fed. Reg. 3967.
14. 323 U.S. 214, 229-230, 65 S.Ct. 193, 200 (1944).
15. *Korematsu* v. *United States*, 323 U.S. 214, 230-231, 65 S.Ct. 193, 200 (1944).
16. *Korematsu* v. *United States*, 323 U.S. 214, 219-220, 65 S.Ct. 193, 195 (1944).
17. *Korematsu* v. *United States*, 323 U.S. 214, 219-220, 65 S.Ct. 193, 195 (1944).
18. *Korematsu* v. *United States*, 323 U.S. 214, 224-225, 65 S.Ct. 193, 197 (1944).
19. *Korematsu* v. *United States*, 323 U.S. 214, 231, 65 S.Ct. 193, 201 (1944).
20. *Korematsu* v. *United States*, 323 U.S. 214, 233, 65 S.Ct. 193, 202 (1944).
21. *Korematsu* v. *United States*, 323 U.S. 214, 233, 65 S.Ct. 193, 202 (1944).
22. *Korematsu* v. *United States*, 323 U.S. 214, 239, 65 S.Ct. 193, 204 (1944).
23. *Selective Draft Law Cases*, 245 U.S. 366, 38 S.Ct. 159 (1918).
24. *Selective Draft Law Cases*, 245 U.S. 366, 377, 38 S.Ct. 159, 161 (1918).
25. *Selective Draft Law Cases*, 245 U.S. 366, 378, 38 S.Ct. 159, 161 (1918).
26. *Selective Draft Law Cases*, 245 U.S. 366, 389-390, 38 S.Ct. 159, 165 (1918).
27. *Bailey* v. *Alabama*, 219 U.S. 219, 240-241, 31 S.Ct. 145, 151 (1911).
28. *Selective Draft Law Cases*, 245 U.S. 366, 378, 38 S.Ct. 159, 161 (1918).
29. *Selective Draft Law Cases*, 245 U.S. 366, 378, 38 S.Ct. 159, 161 (1918).
30. *Selective Draft Law Cases*, 245 U.S. 366, 378, 38 S.Ct. 159, 161 (1918).
31. *Dred Scott* v. *Sanford*, 19 How. (60 U.S.) 393, 403 (1857).
32. *Dred Scott* v. *Sanford*, 19 How. (60 U.S.) 393, 404-405 (1857).
33. *Dred Scott* v. *Sanford*, 19 How. (60 U.S.) 393, 407 (1857).
34. *Dred Scott* v. *Sanford*, 19 How. (60 U.S.) 393, 416 (1857).
35. *Dred Scott* v. *Sanford*, 19 How. (60 U.S.) 393, 426 (1856).
36. 3 Stat. 548, March 6, 1820.
37. *Dred Scott* v. *Sanford*, 19 How. (60 U.S.) 393, 450 (1857).

Chapter 8

1. *Monongahela Navigation Co.* v. *United States*, 148 U.S. 312, 324 (1893).
2. *Calder* v. *Bull*, 3 Dallas (U.S.) 386, 394 (1798), by Justice Chase; emphasis added.
3. *Calder* v. *Bull*, 3 Dallas (U.S.) 386, 399 (1798), by Justice Iredell.

INDEX

abortion
  in Texas, 105
  Roe v. *Wade*, 113-114
Agins v. *City of Tiburon*
  in general, 37-38
Agricultural Adjustment Act
  concerning farmers, 13-14
  passage of, 12
  purpose of, 13
  use of, 13
Alberts v. *California*
  statement by Brennan, 75-76
altruism
  definition of, 5
amendments to U.S. Constitution
  to protect rights, 146
  to violate rights, 146
Arizona
  sodomy laws in, 94
Articles of Confederation
  slavery, 135

Barnett, Walter
  Sexual Freedom & the Constitution:
    An Inquiry into the Constitution-
    ality of Repressive Sex Laws, 93
bigamy
  punishment for, 56
bill of rights
  absence in U.S. Constitution, 140
  argument against, 141-142
  effect on contraceptives, 142
  necessity for, 140, 147
birth control
  banning of, in Laos, 92
  Papal encyclical prohibiting, 99
Black, Hugo
  dissent in *Poe* v. *Ullman*, 104
  on contraceptives, 142
  on obscenity, 77
  opinion in *Braunfeld* v. *Brown*, 62
  opinion in *Korematsu* v. *United*
    States, 122-123

Blackmun, Harry A.
  opinion in *Fullilove* v. *Klutznick*, 23
  opinion in *Paris Adult Theater I* v.
    Slayton, 87
  opinion in *Roe* v. *Wade*, 105, 106,
    107, 108, 109
Blue Laws
  definition of, 58
  effect on religion, 58
Braunfeld v. *Brown*
  implications of, 64
  in general, 58-64
Breard v. *Alexandria*
  compared to *Martin* v. *Struthers*, 70
Brennan, William J.
  dissent in *Braunfeld* v. *Brown*, 62-63
  dissent in *Miller* v. *California*, 89
  dissent in *Paris Adult Theater I* v. *Slay-*
    ton, 88, 89
  on obscenity, 77
  opinion in *Fullilove* v. *Klutznick*, 23
  opinion in *Gallagher* v. *Crown Kosher*
    Super Market of Massachusetts,
    Inc., 63
  opinion in *Griswold* v. *Connecticut*,
    100-101
  opinion in *Roe* v. *Wade*, 105
  opinion in *Roth* v. *United States* and
    Alberts v. *California*, 74-76
Buck v. *Bell*
  as precedent to *Skinner* v. *Oklahoma*,
    117
  in general, 114-117
Burger, Warren
  opinion in *Fullilove* v. *Klutznick*, 23
  opinion in *Miller* v. *California*, 79-80
  opinion in *Paris Adult Theater I* v. *Slay-*
    ton, 79-80, 83, 84, 85, 86, 87
  opinion in *Roe* v. *Wade*, 105
Butler v. *Perry*
  general discussion of case, 118-119